Growing Informal Cities Project

# Informal Migrant Entrepreneurship and Inclusive Growth in South Africa, Zimbabwe and Mozambique

Jonathan Crush, Caroline Skinner and Abel Chikanda

Migration Policy Series No. 68

Series Editor:
Prof. Jonathan Crush

Southern African Migration Programme (SAMP)
International Migration Research Centre (IMRC)
2015

## ACKNOWLEDGEMENTS

We wish to thank the International Development Research Centre (IDRC) for funding the Growing Informal Cities Project, a partnership between SAMP, the African Centre for Cities (UCT), the International Migration Research Centre (Balsillie School of International Affairs), the Gauteng City Regional Observatory and Eduardo Mondlane University (Mozambique). Our thanks to Bronwen Dachs for her assistance with this report.

# CONTENTS                                                         PAGE

# LIST OF TABLES                                                    PAGE

## LIST OF FIGURES        PAGE

# EXECUTIVE SUMMARY

While increasing attention is being paid to the drivers and forms of entrepreneurship in informal economies, much less of this policy and research focus is directed at understanding the links between mobility and informality. This report examines the current state of knowledge about this relationship with particular reference to three countries (Mozambique, South Africa and Zimbabwe) and four cities (Cape Town, Harare, Johannesburg and Maputo), identifying major themes, knowledge gaps, research questions and policy implications. In many African cities, informal enterprises are operated by internal and international migrants. The extent and nature of mobile entrepreneurship and the opportunities and challenges confronting migrant entrepreneurs are under-researched in Africa in general and Southern Africa in particular. Their contribution to the informal economy and employment generation in countries of destination and origin are similarly undervalued by policy-makers. Informal migrant entrepreneurs are often viewed with suspicion, if not hostility, by citizens and officials. In part, this is because central and municipal governments see them as increasing the growth of an informal sector that they want tamed, if not eradicated. Also, it is because they are often incorrectly seen as all "illegal immigrants" and, by definition, engaged in illicit activities. And, in countries with high levels of xenophobia such as South Africa, migrant-owned businesses are a visible and easy target for xenophobic attacks. Violent attacks on migrant entrepreneurs and their property have become extremely common in many South African cities.

South Africa's relatively small informal sector is accompanied by very high unemployment levels. Many commentators therefore feel that the South African informal economy ought to be much larger than it is. Given the apartheid-era repression of informal entrepreneurship, the key question may not be why the informal economy is not larger, but why, after decades of repression, it is as large and important as it is. One of the reasons is that the informal economy is not just populated by South African citizens. Migrants from other African countries play an increasingly important role in the sector and experience considerable success, something that eludes many locally-owned start-ups. Informal retailing has been the major focus of economic research on different sub-sectors of the informal economy. Particularly common are small-area case studies of survivalist street trading (particularly of food and handicrafts) in the inner city. The spaza shop sector in low-income residential areas has also been studied. Other informal entrepreneurial activities that have attracted attention include the minibus taxi industry, waste collection and recycling, shebeens, trade in medicinal plants and poverty tourism.

As well as documenting the economic challenges of informality, the existing literature on the South African informal economy raises two other important issues that have a bearing on the environment for entrepreneurship. The first is the relationship between formal and informal retail. The central research question is whether the rapid expansion of malls and supermarkets across the South African urban landscape, and their recent penetration of low-income areas, is having a negative impact on the informal economy. The second issue concerns the formalization of informal businesses, partially due to the ILO's 2014-15 standard-setting process on "Formalizing the Informal Economy." For reasons including greater legal control, collection of taxes and registration fees, enforcement of labour legislation and identification and deportation of irregular migrants, the South African authorities would like to see the informal economy subject to formal rules and regulations. In South Africa, the drive towards formalization has progressed furthest in the taxi industry but many sectors of the informal economy remain outside the regulatory fold. Most informal entrepreneurs are opposed to formalization, stressing the financial costs and constraints on business flexibility.

The Zimbabwean experience raises important questions about the links between the collapse of the formal economy and the growth of informality. At independence in 1980, Zimbabwe's urban informal economy was small, absorbing about 10% of the labour force. By 2003, it accounted for over 70% of the labour force and its contribution to gross national income (GNI) had grown to around 60%. In 2011, 84% of the workforce were in informal employment. The largest number were in retail and wholesale trade followed by repair of motor vehicles and cycles, services and manufacturing. Women constituted 53% of those in informal employment. There have been few studies of the impact of state failure on the urban informal economy. Yet, under conditions of economic crisis, participation in more lucrative income-generating activities in the informal sector becomes essential and there are strong indications that the collapse of the economy actually had a positive impact on Zimbabweans' entrepreneurial motivations and skills.

Mozambique represents a different scenario in terms of the links between informal entrepreneurship and formal economic growth. The Mozambican economy was virtually destroyed by the civil war in the 1980s and the vast majority of urban residents managed to survive through the informal economy. In the last two decades, Mozambique has had one of the fastest-growing formal economies in Africa. Yet, the informal economy has proven to be extremely resilient. A 2005 survey concluded that 75% of the economically-active population was employed informally in Mozambique. Another survey of Maputo found that 70% of the city's households are involved in informal economic activities and about 65% of jobs are in the informal economy. Although research on the informal economy is not as extensive as in Zimbabwe or South African cities, several studies have highlighted the dynamism and heterogeneity of the sector and the role of informal entrepreneurship in poverty reduction. The most common type of informal economic activity is the sale of foodstuffs and petty commodities.

Mobility is essential to the urban informal economy in Southern African cities. Within urban areas, mobility is a vital component of the business strategies of informal operatives who identify spaces with niche markets or a relative absence of the formal sector. While some businesses operate from fixed sites, others use different parts of the city on different days or at different times of a single day. Many participants in the informal economy are internal or international migrants, often in competition with one another for the same market share. Although the numbers of international migrants are frequently exaggerated, it is clear that they have played an increasingly important role in the informal economies of Southern African cities over the last two decades and have reshaped the nature of informality and informal entrepreneurship in the region. Yet the importance of that role is often underestimated, invisible to researchers and denigrated by policy-makers.

Recent studies of migrant entrepreneurship in South Africa focus on several key issues:

- Migration histories and the demographic profile of migrant entrepreneurs;
- The activities and business strategies of migrant entrepreneurs;
- The ethnic networks that enable access to resources such as business capital, cost-saving strategies such as shared shop spaces, revenue-boosting strategies such as bulk buying, and material support such as accommodation for newly-arrived migrants;
- The institutionalized xenophobia and routine criminal violence that are a constant threat to migrant business activity;
- The entrepreneurial orientation and motivation of migrant business owners;
- The gendered character of migrant entrepreneurial opportunity and activity; and
- The regulatory framework governing informality and migrant entrepreneurship.

Migrants are often more entrepreneurial than most, yet the constraints they face in establishing and growing their businesses are considerable. Their general contribution to employment creation and inclusive growth is undervalued and often misrepresented as a threat. Foreign migrants in the South African informal economy do have considerable entrepreneurial ambition but are severely hampered in growing their enterprises by obstacles including:

- National immigration and refugee policies, which determine the terms and conditions of entry and the ability to move along migration corridors between countries;
- Documentation, which determines the degree of access to social, financial and support services;

- Immigration law enforcement, with the ever-present threat of arrest and deportation disrupting business activity;
- Lack of access to credit (refugees and asylum seekers are commonly refused bank accounts and loans);
- Municipal regulations, which are generally unfriendly to the informal sector, and hostile and xenophobic local attitudes.

Violent attacks on the persons and properties of migrant business operations – whether motivated by rivalry, criminality or xenophobia or a combination of these – are regular and frequent and involve considerable loss of property and life.

In terms of economic challenges confronting informal-sector entrepreneurs, both South African and migrant, a major issue is the lack of access to financial services including start-up capital and ongoing credit. Formal financial institutions are extremely reluctant to do business with migrant informal entrepreneurs. As a result, many rely on various financial bootstrapping alternatives to minimize their capital outlay and running costs. Despite these financial challenges, there is evidence of upward mobility of migrant-owned businesses in terms of the growth of business capital. A central premise of the hostility towards foreign migrants in South Africa is that they "steal" jobs from South Africans. However, the studies reviewed in this report suggest the opposite. Migrant entrepreneurs certainly create employment opportunities for other migrants but they also hire many South Africans. More research is needed, however, on why migrant entrepreneurs employ South Africans and under what conditions. The essence of an inclusive-growth perspective on informality is that the sector should create "decent" jobs. Whether or not the jobs created deserve this label has yet to be established.

Among the most common manifestations of mobile informality in Southern Africa are the inter-urban linkages across international boundaries. When it comes to relations between South Africa, Mozambique and Zimbabwe, most of this business is conducted by individuals travelling overland and engaged in so-called ICBT (informal cross-border trade). ICBT plays a vital, though largely unrecognized, role in regional economic integration and in linking informal economies in different SADC cities. Informal traders need to be seen as entrepreneurs and their activities as a potentially strong promoter of inclusive growth and employment creation across the region. In Mozambique and Zimbabwe, a sizeable number of informal entrepreneurs are international migrants. They establish their businesses in their home cities, such as Maputo and Harare, and grow them by taking advantage of the opportunities provided by cross-border economic linkages and migration. Informal cross-border traders, many of them women, thus play a critical role in the circulation of formally and informally produced goods throughout the SADC region.

A related aspect of the relationship between migration and informal entrepreneurship is the massive flow of cash remittances and goods that migrants in Johannesburg and Cape Town send to Mozambique and Zimbabwe, including the cities of Maputo and Harare. The use of formal channels for remittance transfers is very limited in both Mozambique and Zimbabwe. The business opportunities for small-scale entrepreneurs in the remittances industry are largely in the channels through which remittances of cash and goods are sent home by migrants. Informal transport operators called the *Omalayisha* move cash, people and consumer goods between Zimbabwe and South Africa, for example.

Gender issues are of particular relevance in understanding the nature of informal enterprise in Southern African cities. Cross-border migration has always been highly gendered in the region. The feminization of migration is well under way with the numbers and proportion of female migrants to South Africa increasing rapidly. Unable to obtain work permits, many women are hired as irregular migrants, which heightens their vulnerability. Others are forced into survivalist activities in the urban informal economy. In both Harare and Maputo, gender-based tussles characterize the informal economy. The collapse of the formal economy pushed many more men into the sector and made the highly competitive informal business environment a site of new conflict. Cross-border trade between Zimbabwe, Mozambique and South Africa was initially dominated by women but high rates of unemployment amongst men have prompted them to move into the trade, leading to growing gender conflict over control of sectors of the trade and the proceeds of trade.

These gender-based issues can be reformulated as a set of key research questions: (a) does the feminization of migration impact on the nature of participation of women in the informal economy, are there gender differences in the types and opportunities for involvement of men and women in informal entrepreneurship and does small business development offer women (and especially women-headed households) a way out of urban poverty? (b) what kinds of challenges affect migrant female and not male entrepreneurs and what strategies do they adopt to establish and grow their businesses? (c) how do intra-household gender roles and expectations impact on the ability of women to establish and grow their informal enterprises? and (d) are national and local policies on migration and the informal economy disadvantageous to female entrepreneurs and what kinds of policy reforms would mitigate this situation?

Participation in the informal economy may be enforced, in the sense that there are no alternatives, but that does not mean that all participants are therefore just "getting by" until a better opportunity presents itself in the formal economy. One of the most vexing questions for small-business advocates in South Africa is what is commonly seen as an underdeveloped entrepreneurial motivation or "spirit" amongst those living in more disadvantaged areas of the country. Some studies have contested this stereotype while others have sought explanations that are lodged in the repressive legacy of apartheid and the dysfunctional South African education system. The perception that migrants are far more successful entrepreneurs than South Africans in the informal economy has prompted a new research focus on migrant entrepreneurial orientation and motivation and favourable comparisons with South African entrepreneurs. Migrants tend to score better than South Africans on various indicators of entrepreneurial orientation including achievement, innovation, personal initiative and "competitive intelligence."

The three countries (and four municipalities) discussed in this report represent contrasting policy responses to the informal economy and informal migrant entrepreneurship. The predominant attitude towards the informal economy in Zimbabwe over the last decade has been extremely negative and at odds with the reality of survival in a rapidly shrinking formal economy with mass unemployment. These views culminated in the nationwide assault on informality through Operation Murambatsvina (Clean Out the Trash) in 2005, which attempted to destroy all manifestations of urban informality: businesses, markets and shelter. Murambatsvina temporarily devastated the informal economy and the livelihoods of the urban poor in many Zimbabwean cities but informality quickly rebounded and returned to the urban spaces from which it had been erased. If Zimbabwe's economic recovery continues, it is important to know whether the state will adopt a more tolerant approach to informality or whether the vast informal economy will continue to "fly under the radar" and be the target of repression.

In Mozambique, national and municipal authorities have traditionally adopted a tolerant approach to the informal economy. While it has been subject to periodic harassment, it is generally viewed within official circles as an important and sustainable source of livelihood for the urban poor. The policy aim is not to eliminate informality but to "discourage" illegality through registration and formalization. One mechanism has been the establishment of formal urban markets where vendors pay rent for stands. However, many of these stands remain unoccupied. In 2008, a simplified tax for small businesses was introduced, payable as a percentage of turnover or as a lump sum. However, uptake has been low. Informal entrepreneurs have been largely resistant to such efforts, which are viewed as a "money grab by the state." There is some evidence that operators who have registered and paid licences and taxes are more productive than those who spend a great deal of effort evading the authorities, but the obstacles to formalization and why this might be avoided or resisted need further research, as do the implications of formalization.

The South African response to informality lies somewhere between the Mozambican and Zimbabwean, but has been neither consistent nor coherent. At the national level, recent initiatives illustrate the kinds of anti-foreign thinking that inform the national government's policy response. The National Informal Business Upliftment Strategy was launched in 2013 focusing on skills development, product improvement, technology support, equipment, and help with registration. The stated target of business upliftment is entrepreneurial activity in the informal economy. However, it also expresses clear anti-foreign sentiments. Another was the tabling in Parliament of the draconian Licensing of Businesses Bill in 2013. The Bill is extremely punitive and would result in large-scale criminalization of current informal activities. It also suggests that community-based organizations, non-governmental organizations and others will be given the job of working with the licensing authorities to police non-South African businesses. The xenophobic attacks of 2008 demonstrated that there are elements in many communities who need no encouragement to turn on their neighbours from other African countries.

At the local level, in both Cape Town and Johannesburg, there are contradictions between policy statements affirming the positive contribution of the informal economy and the actual implementation of policy. In late 2013, the Johannesburg City Council violently removed and confiscated the inventory of an estimated 6,000 inner-city street traders, many of them migrants. The City has commissioned a project to consider alternatives to informality while simultaneously pursuing the declaration of large inner city areas restricted and prohibited trade zones. Recent research on inner-city Cape Town suggests that there is less violent but more systemic exclusion and there is evidence of ongoing harassment of traders throughout the city. Some of the most dedicated, enterprising and successful entrepreneurs in the South African informal economy are migrants to the country. Under any other circumstances they would probably be lauded by government as examples of successful small-scale micro-entrepreneurship. However, the state and many citizens view their activities as highly undesirable simply because of their national origins. Harassment, extortion and bribery of officialdom are some of the daily costs of doing business in South Africa. Many entrepreneurs, especially in informal settlements and townships, face constant security threats and enjoy minimal protection from the police.

The Growing Informal Cities (GIC) project is examining and profiling the "hidden" role of migrant informal entrepreneurship in different Southern African cities. The cities were chosen for analysis and comparison because they represent different forms of migrant entrepreneurship. In South African cities like Cape Town and Johannesburg, migrant entrepreneurs come from throughout Africa including Zimbabwe and Mozambique. In Maputo and Harare, most migrant entrepreneurs are local but they structure their businesses around the opportunities afforded by growing regional integration and cross-border migration to and from South Africa. Policies towards informality and informal entrepreneurship vary from country to country. In Zimbabwe, the informal economy has been ruthlessly repressed but survives nonetheless. In Mozambique, there is a laissez-faire attitude towards the informal economy and attempts to formalize informal businesses through registration have not been particularly successful. In South Africa, informality is generally encouraged at the national level through training programmes and support activities. But at the municipal level, the informal economy is often viewed in negative terms and pathologized. The impacts of national and municipal programmes and actions are uncertain especially for migrant entrepreneurs. Indeed, these entrepreneurs, who could and do contribute to inclusive growth, are subjected to social and economic exclusion which spills over into xenophobia.

The GIC project is generating a comparative body of knowledge about informal migrant entrepreneurs, raising their profile in regional, national and municipal policy debates with a view to effecting positive change in the regulatory environment in which they operate. By allowing migrant entrepreneurs to expand and reach their full potential, free of harassment and exclusion, a major contribution can be made to facilitating inclusive growth through informal entrepreneurship. To this end, GIC is advancing understanding of the reciprocal links between mobility and informal entrepreneurship in Southern African cities through a programme of rigorous research oriented to the economic growth and poverty reduction goals of SADC governments, and impacting on policy implementation processes around migration, development and urban management.

# INTRODUCTION

Cities in the South will absorb 95% of urban growth in the next two decades and by 2030 will be home to almost 4 billion people (or 80% of the world's urban population).[1] Urban growth will be most intense in the cities of Asia and Africa. Over half of the population of the African continent will be living in urban areas by 2030 (or an estimated 750 million people). Southern Africa is one of the fastest-urbanizing regions in the world.[2] The region currently has a population of approximately 210 million, at least 100 million of whom live in urban and peri-urban areas. More than 60% of the population of two countries (Botswana and South Africa) is already urbanized.[3] By mid-century, 11 countries are projected to have more urban than rural dwellers (Figure 1). More than half of the overall regional population already live in urban areas, a figure projected to rise to three-quarters by 2050. With rapid urbanization and persistent urban poverty, urban development challenges are set to intensify.[4]

**Figure 1: Current and Projected Urbanization in SADC Countries**

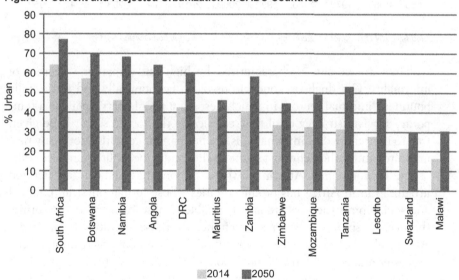

*Source: Adapted from UN Department of Economic and Social Affairs[5]*

**Figure 2: Southern Africa Urban Population Growth, 1950-2050**

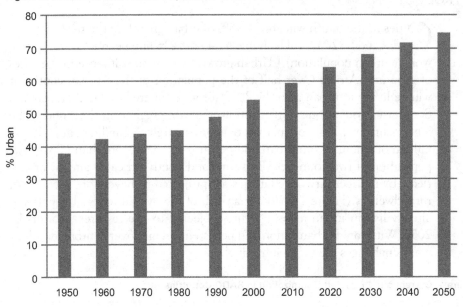

*Source: Adapted from UN Department of Economic and Social Affairs, Population Division (2014)[6]*

The African city is characterized by high and expanding degrees of informality. Old dualistic conceptions of an economically and territorially bounded "informal sector" in which desperate people participate as a temporary survival strategy until they can access the formal sector have given way to the reality that informality is the permanent condition for many new urbanites and is the defining feature of the landscape, politics and economy of the contemporary African city.[7] As Simone has argued, "accelerated urbanization in Africa has produced cities whose formal physical, political and social infrastructures are largely unable to absorb, apprehend or utilize the needs, aspirations and resourcefulness of those who live within them. As a result, the efforts to secure livelihoods depend on largely informalized processes and a wide range of provisional and ephemeral institutions which cultivate specific orientations toward, knowledge of, and practices for, dealing with urban life. Soon, the majority of Africans will live in peri-urban and informal settlements often at the physical, if not necessarily social, margins of the city."[8]

The extent and importance of informality in African cities and to African economies is subject to widely varying estimates. The Economic Commission for Africa recently noted, for example, that "informal trade is as old as the informal economy. It is the main source of job creation in Africa, providing between 20 per cent and 75 per cent of total employment in most countries."[9] In most African cities, informality is the "main game in town."[10]

Yet, as Potts notes, the lack of adequate data about informality "is scarcely surprising as one defining feature is that it is unregistered, and very loose treatment of the issue of 'underemployment' which often gets classified, erroneously, as unemployment."[11] The International Labour Organization (ILO) and the research-policy network Women in Informal Employment: Globalizing and Organizing (WIEGO) have recently made considerable advances in generating country comparable and regional estimates of the size of the informal economy.[12] Their data shows that informal employment comprises more than half of non-agricultural employment in most regions of the Global South – 82% in South Asia, 66% in Sub-Saharan Africa, 65% in East and Southeast Asia and 51% in Latin America.[13] There is also significant variation between countries. For example, the proportion of non-agricultural work in the informal sector ranges from 18% in South Africa to 40% in Zimbabwe to 71% in Mali (Figure 3).

**Figure 3: Employment in the Informal Sector in Selected African Countries (% of non-agricultural work)**

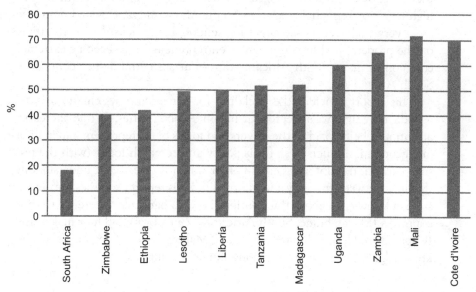

*Source: ILO[14]*

Although the individual incomes of informal workers are often low, cumulatively their activities contribute significantly to gross domestic product (GDP). The ILO has compiled data on the contribution of informal enterprises to national GDP in 16 Sub-Saharan countries and, on average, the informal economy contributed 41%.[15] The proportion varied from 58% in Ghana to 24% in Zambia. A more recent ILO publication provides evidence of the contribution of the informal economy to the GDP of a smaller number of countries. It finds, for example, that in Benin, Niger and Togo, the informal economy contributes more than 50% of non-agricultural GDP.[16] These figures show that the informal economy not only plays an important employment generation and poverty alleviation role, but is critical to local economies.

In many African cities, informal enterprises are operated by internal and international migrants. The extent and nature of mobile entrepreneurship and the opportunities and challenges confronting migrant entrepreneurs are under-researched in Africa in general and Southern Africa in particular.[17] Their contribution to the informal economy and employment generation in countries of destination and origin are similarly undervalued by policy-makers. Informal migrant entrepreneurs are often viewed with suspicion, if not outright hostility, by citizenries and officialdom. In part, this is because central and municipal governments see them as increasing the growth of an informal sector that they would rather see tamed or eradicated. Also, it is because they are often incorrectly viewed as "illegal migrants" and therefore, by definition, engaged in illicit activities. And, in countries with high levels of xenophobia such as South Africa, migrant-owned businesses are a very visible and easy target for xenophobic attacks.[18] Violent attacks on the property and lives of migrant entrepreneurs have become extremely common in many South African cities – but are certainly not confined to South Africa.[19]

This report provides the backdrop for a new and systematic research agenda on migrant entrepreneurship in African cities. While increasing attention is being paid to the drivers and forms of entrepreneurship in informal economies, much less of this policy and research focus (with the possible exception of informal cross-border trade) is directed at understanding the links between mobility and informality. This report examines the current state of knowledge about this relationship with particular reference to three countries (Mozambique, South Africa and Zimbabwe) and four major cities (Cape Town, Harare, Johannesburg and Maputo), identifying major themes, knowledge gaps, research questions and policy implications.

## URBANIZATION AND INFORMALITY

In Southern Africa, differences in the countries and cities of South Africa, Zimbabwe and Mozambique allow a comparative exploration of the links between the informal economy, entrepreneurship and inclusive growth. South Africa has the largest formal economy in the region but a relatively small informal sector. Statistics South Africa's (SSA) 2014 April to June Quarterly Labour Force Survey recorded 2,379,000 people working in the informal sector.[20] This constitutes only 16.5% of non-agricultural employment.[21] The South African informal sector is dominated by wholesale and retail trade (44%), community and social services (15%) and construction (15%). Unlike in many other developing countries, only a small group of people are involved in manufacturing (10%).[22] Another unusual feature of the South African informal economy is its gender composition. In the majority of Sub-Saharan African countries, the percentage of women in the informal sector is much higher than men; however, in South Africa more men than women work in the informal sector.[23] In Quarter 1 (2008), 46% of those reporting that they worked in the informal sector were women while by Quarter 4 (2014) this percentage was down to 40%, suggesting rapid change.[24]

South Africa's small informal sector is accompanied by very high unemployment levels. The latest available SSA figures recorded 5,154,000 people as unemployed, while a further 2,419,000 were recorded as "discouraged" job seekers.[25] Combined, this constitutes 33.4% of the labour force.[26] Many commentators therefore feel that the South African informal economy ought to be much larger. What is sometimes forgotten, however, is that until the 1990s the informal economy was viewed by apartheid policymakers as "an ominous and unpleasant aberration (and) a blot on the urban landscape." The overwhelming policy thrust was "towards repression of small-scale enterprises, seeking their excision from the urban landscape."[27] Given this apartheid legacy and associated hostility towards informality, the key question may not be why the informal economy is not larger, but why, after decades of repression, it is as large and important as it is. That said, a body of research is emerging that looks at the barriers to self-employment in contemporary South African cities. These include crime, the risk of business failure, lack of start-up capital, high transport costs and social disincentives.[28]

Data for the Quarterly Labour Force Survey is gathered in such a way that city-level statistics are unreliable. Disaggregation by province suggests that the size and nature of the informal sector differs significantly. In the two most industrialized and urbanized provinces, the Western Cape and Gauteng, the informal sector is relatively small (at 11% and 14% of non-agricultural employment respectively).[29] This contrasts with Limpopo where 32% of non-agricultural work is in the informal sector. The Gauteng City-Region Observatory's Quality of Life Survey of 2013 interviewed a representative sample of residents and suggests a bigger informal sector in the region, however.[30] Twenty-two percent of respondents who were employed worked in the informal sector and 27% of respondent households received some income from the informal sector. The main difficulty with employment figures, of course, is that they inevitably include both business owners and employees. The actual number of enterprises is more difficult to gauge, especially as business failure is high and turnover common.[31] A panel survey of 300 informal businesses in Soweto, for example, found that

55% of those operating in 2007 had failed by 2010.[32] In 2004, the Bureau for Market Research estimated that there were 748,700 informal outlets in the country including 261,000 hawkers, 127,600 spaza shops, 40,100 shebeens and 320,000 other types of businesses.[33]

Informal retailing has been the major focus of economic research on different sub-sectors of the informal economy in both Johannesburg and Cape Town.[34] Particularly common are small-area case studies of survivalist street trading (particularly of food and handicrafts) in the inner city.[35] The spaza shop sector in low-income residential areas has also been increasingly studied.[36] Other informal entrepreneurial activities that have attracted attention in Cape Town and Johannesburg include the minibus taxi industry,[37] waste collection and recycling,[38] shebeen operation,[39] trade in medicinal plants,[40] poverty tourism[41] and informal construction activity.[42] Methodologically, an interesting approach to understanding the complexity and dynamics of informal retail has been the use of GIS to map the spatial distribution of informal retail outlets and to relate this to other urban features such as the transportation infrastructure and the location of competitor formal retailers.[43]

As well as documenting the economic challenges of informality, the literature on Cape Town and Johannesburg raises two other important issues, both of which have a bearing on the environment for entrepreneurship. The first is the relationship between formal and informal retail. The linkages between formal and informal enterprise are often overlooked in the conventional dualistic model that undergirds much analysis of a functionally and spatially bounded informal sector.[44] With regard to the issue of economic competition, the central research question is whether the rapid expansion of malls and supermarkets across the South African urban landscape, and their recent penetration of low-income areas, is having a negative impact on the informal economy.[45] One study, for example, has argued that "one of the primary threats is the encroachment of supermarkets into areas traditionally occupied by the informal market. There is, for example, strong evidence that the informal sector is losing significant market share as a result of the encroachment of supermarkets into the territories occupied by the informal sector."[46] The study reports that between 2003 and 2005, spaza shop turnover in some areas was reduced by as much as 22% as a result. In contrast, a study of Tshwane argues that supermarkets have had a major impact on corner stores and greengrocers but that informal vendors are far more resilient.[47]

Studies in Soweto have found that the impact varies with the type of informal business: although spazas and general dealers were negatively affected by the advent of malls, street traders were not.[48] In nearby Ekurhuleni, however, formal retail dominates the informal food economy because the latter's collective buying power is not being used in the same way as large formal retailers of fruit and vegetables to obtain better terms of trade with suppliers.[49] The African Food Security Urban Network (AFSUN) data for Cape Town and Johannesburg shows that the majority of poor urban households source food from both supermarkets (for staples in bulk on a monthly basis) and informal vendors (for street food and fresh produce several times a week).[50] The possibility of corporate social responsibility programmes being directed to supporting informal entrepreneurs has recently been mooted. One study concludes that "business development support has a positive effect on lifting income and reducing poverty for microenterprise owners."[51]

Formalization of informal businesses is the other issue that has become increasingly important in South Africa. This has been given greater profile in part due to the ILO's 2014-15 standard-setting process on "Formalizing the Informal Economy." For reasons including greater legal control, collection of taxes and registration fees, enforcement of labour legislation and identification and deportation of irregular migrants running businesses, the central, provincial and local South African authorities would all like to see the informal economy subject to formal rules and regulations. Many researchers see formalization as good for informal business since it would promote access to private finance and state-funded training programmes.[52] Chen does caution that "it is important to ensure that formalization offers the benefits and protections that come with being formal and does not simply impose the costs of becoming formal." She also notes that formalization has different meanings and implications for different categories of informal workers.[53] In South Africa, the drive towards formalization has progressed furthest in the taxi industry but many sectors of the informal economy remain outside the formal regulatory fold. Most informal entrepreneurs are opposed to formalization, stressing the financial costs and constraints on business flexibility. Attempts by the state to promote formalization in the liquor sector have led, perhaps counterintuitively, to greater informalization.[54]

The Zimbabwean experience raises important questions about the links between the collapse of the formal economy and the growth of informality.[55] At independence in 1980, Zimbabwe's urban informal economy was small, absorbing about 10% of the labour force. By 2003, it accounted for over 70% of the labour force and its contribution to GNI had grown to around 60% – one of the highest in Sub-Saharan Africa.[56] In Harare, the informal economy rapidly expanded even as the formal economy shrank and rates of unemployment soared above 80%.[57] In 2011, a ZimStat survey found that 84% of the workforce were in informal employment. The largest number were in retail and wholesale trade followed by repair of motor vehicles and cycles, services and manufacturing. Women constituted 53% of those in informal employment.[58] There have been few studies (in Zimbabwe and elsewhere) of the impact of state failure on the urban informal economy.

Yet, as Dube points out, under conditions of economic crisis and state failure there are "many business opportunities that may arise and being tied to an employer in the formal sector may preclude an entrepreneurial worker's participation in more lucrative income generating activities in the informal sector."[59]

There are strong indications that the collapse of the Zimbabwean economy actually impacted positively on the entrepreneurial motivations and skills of ordinary Zimbabweans.[60] One case study has suggested that after 2004 there was a major shift within the informal economy from household informal employment towards small enterprise development and employment.[61] At the very least this points to the informal economy not as a site of desperation and last resort but a space of energy and innovation. As Dube concludes, "instead of treating the informal sector as an undifferentiated residual sector, there is a need for studies on informality in Zimbabwe that disaggregate this sector by sub-sector of activities and by locales – examining differences in activities, barriers to entry/exit and employment relationships in the various sub-sectors and/or locales."[62]

Mozambique, and Maputo in particular, represent a different context within which to explore the links between informal entrepreneurship and formal economic growth. The Mozambican economy was virtually destroyed by the civil war in the 1980s and the informal economy was how the vast majority of urban residents managed to survive.[63] In the last two decades, however, Mozambique has had one of the fastest growing formal economies in Africa. Yet, the informal economy has proven to be extremely resilient. The Ministry of Planning and Development, for example, estimated that informal activity represented 41% of GDP in 2003 and 40% in 2004.[64] A 2005 national sample survey concluded that 75% of the economically active population was employed informally in Mozambique. Another survey of Maputo found that 70% of households were involved in informal economic activities and 64% of jobs were estimated to be in the informal economy. The involvement was significantly higher in female-headed households (86%) than male-headed households (62%).[65]

Although research on the informal economy in Maputo is not as extensive as in Harare or South African cities such as Johannesburg, a number of studies have highlighted the dynamism and heterogeneity of the sector and the role of informal entrepreneurship in poverty reduction.[66] The most common type of informal economic activity is the sale of products such as foodstuffs and petty commodities. Many are also involved in *desenrascar* ("finding a way out"), which involves everything from small-scale repairs to sex work and theft. The most profitable activities are hairdressing, the sale of second-hand clothes and traditional medicine. Other common informal activities include the sale of water, production of building material and furniture, garbage picking, selling cell-phone airtime and the sale of charcoal and home-made brews.[67]

## INTERNATIONAL MIGRATION IN SOUTHERN AFRICA

The end of apartheid brought a major reconfiguration of international migration flows in Southern Africa.[68] Legal entries through South African land border posts and airports rose from less than 1 million in 1990 to 6 million in 2000, and 15 million in 2014.[69] These entrants (totalling nearly 130 million from 2000 to 2013) include tourists, visitors, migrant workers, immigrants, students, medical travellers, shoppers, investors, conference delegates, diplomats, asylum-seekers and informal traders. Among the entrants are those who give one purpose for entry (for example, holiday) and then engage in other activities, such as working in the informal economy. The vast majority of those who enter do so on a temporary basis, although there is some discrepancy in official statistics between arrivals and departures each year (Figure 4). The departure figures are likely to be a serious underestimate as exits are not tracked as conscientiously as entries.[70] This clearly shows the problems associated with the exit data. At the Zimbabwean border, for example, busloads of passengers are often simply waved through by South African immigration officials.[71] However, arrivals data also includes many non-visitors.

**Figure 4: South African Arrivals and Departures, 2000-2013**

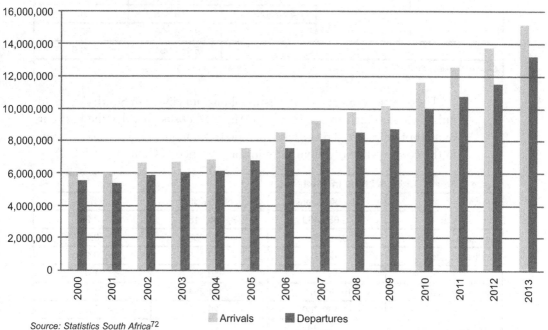

Source: Statistics South Africa[72]

Data collected by Statistics South Africa on foreign arrivals is split into two categories: non-visitors (e.g. temporary or permanent migrants, labour migrants, asylum seekers, students) and visitors (same-day visitors and tourists). Of the 15,154,991 people who visited South Africa in 2013, 837,083

(5.5%) were non-visitors while 14,317,908 (94.5%) were visitors (Table 1). The visitors were made up of 4,781,340 same-day visitors and 9,536,568 overnight visitors or tourists. The vast majority of the same-day visitors (98%) came by road from neighbouring SADC countries and 69% of the tourists also came from SADC countries, including Zimbabwe (20.3% of the total number of tourists), Lesotho (15.3%), Mozambique (11.7%), Swaziland (8.8%) and Botswana (5.6%).

| Table 1: Region of Origin of Visitors to South Africa, 2013 | | | | Number | Percentage |
|---|---|---|---|---|---|
| Non-visitors | | | | 837,083 | 5.5 |
| Visitors | | | | 14,317,908 | 94.5 |
| | Same day | | Overseas | 222,128 | 1.5 |
| | | | SADC | 4,542,149 | 30.0 |
| | | | Other Africa | 13,906 | 0.1 |
| | | | Unspecified | 3,157 | 0.0 |
| | | | Total | 4,781,340 | 31.5 |
| | Tourist | | Overseas | 2,660,631 | 17.6 |
| | | | SADC | 6,618,866 | 43.7 |
| | | | Other Africa | 237,186 | 1.6 |
| | | | Unspecified | 19,885 | 0.1 |
| | | | Total | 9,536,568 | 62.9 |
| Total | | | | 15,154,991 | 100.0 |
| Source: Statistics South Africa[73] | | | | | |

The precise numbers of international migrants living in South Africa are unknown, although the 2011 South African Census provides the best current set of estimates. The Census recorded a total of 1.6 million non-citizens in the country, half of whom were in the province of Gauteng (Table 2).

| Table 2: Foreign Citizens Living in South Africa, 2011 | | | |
|---|---|---|---|
| Province | No. of citizens | No. of non-citizens | % of non-citizens |
| Western Cape | 5,650,462 | 180,815 | 3.2 |
| Eastern Cape | 6,437,586 | 57,938 | 0.9 |
| Northern Cape | 1,125,306 | 10,128 | 0.9 |
| Free State | 2,663,080 | 50,599 | 1.9 |
| KwaZulu-Natal | 10,113,978 | 111,254 | 1.1 |
| North West | 3,439,700 | 120,390 | 3.5 |
| Gauteng | 11,952,392 | 848,620 | 7.1 |
| Mpumalanga | 3,983,570 | 103,573 | 2.6 |
| Limpopo | 5,322,134 | 138,375 | 2.6 |
| Total | 50,688,208 | 1,621,692 | 3.2 |
| Source: Statistics South Africa[74] | | | |

The South African migrant stock (those born outside the country) was dominated by Zimbabweans (a total of 515,000 adults between the ages of 15 and 64) (Table 3). Other countries with 70,000 migrants or more in South Africa include Mozambique, Lesotho and Malawi. The only non-African country in the top 10 is India (at 24,000). Many migrant entrepreneurs in South Africa entered the country as asylum-seekers and later obtained refugee status. The number of asylum applications rose dramatically from around 16,000 in 1996 to a peak of about 220,000 in 2009, primarily as a result of claims submitted by Zimbabweans (Figure 5).

| Table 3: Foreign Migrants Living in South Africa by Country of Birth and Employment Status | | | | |
|---|---|---|---|---|
| | Total | Employment rate (%) | Unemployment rate (%) | Labour force participation rate (%) |
| Zimbabwe | 515,824 | 66 | 18 | 80 |
| Mozambique | 262,556 | 58 | 24 | 76 |
| Lesotho | 124,463 | 51 | 30 | 73 |
| Malawi | 69,544 | 72 | 14 | 84 |
| Namibia | 29,653 | 67 | 10 | 74 |
| Swaziland | 27,471 | 52 | 22 | 67 |
| India | 23,780 | 64 | 6 | 68 |
| Zambia | 22,833 | 70 | 9 | 76 |
| Nigeria | 20,983 | 69 | 13 | 79 |
| Congo | 18,545 | 52 | 24 | 68 |
| Source: Budlender[75] | | | | |

**Figure 5: Applications for Refugee Status in South Africa, 1996-2012**

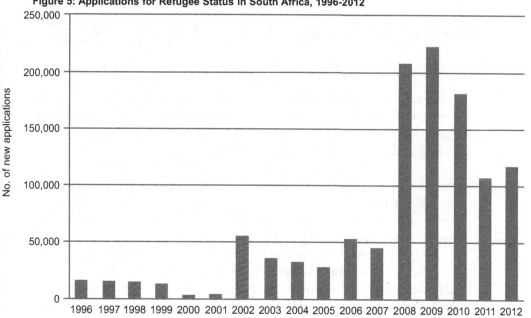

Source: UNHCR Statistical Yearbook (Various Reports)

Migration to South Africa has been the dominant form of movement from post-colonial Zimbabwe, especially for the semi-skilled and unskilled.[76] Movement from Zimbabwe to South Africa has grown rapidly in recent decades (Figure 6). The number of Zimbabweans entering South Africa legally and temporarily for various reasons rose from 255,988 in 1990 to 477,380 in 2000 and to 1,847,973 in 2012. In 2012, the majority of Zimbabweans (97%) indicated holiday as their purpose of entry while other categories included transit (1.5%), business (1%) and study (0.6 %). Many "holiday makers" from Zimbabwe are known to engage in a wide variety of income-generating activities in South Africa, particularly informal trade.

**Figure 6: Legal Entries of Zimbabweans into South Africa, 1980-2012**

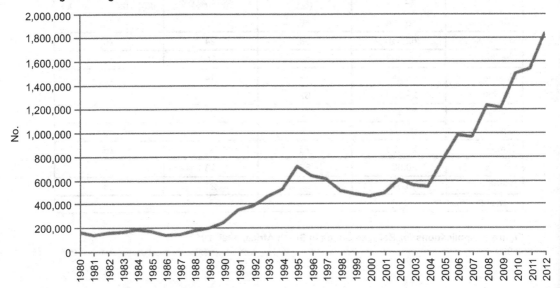

Source: Statistics South Africa, Various reports

In 2001, the South African Census recorded 130,090 Zimbabwe-born people in the country (a figure that included 54,294 whites who had left Zimbabwe after independence in 1980). Only a decade later, the 2011 Census counted a total of 515,824 Zimbabweans aged between 15 and 64 in South Africa.[77] This increase occurred despite a major campaign to deport Zimbabweans, which saw the number of deportees rise from 43,000 in 1999 (or 23% of total deportations) to 205,000 in 2007 (or two-thirds of the total) (Table 4). In total, between 2000 and 2008, nearly 600,000 Zimbabweans were deported from South Africa.

Zimbabwean migrants responded to the mass deportations by applying in large numbers for refugee status in South Africa, which would protect them from deportation. The number of refugee claimants rose from just four in 2001 to 149,453 in 2009 (Figure 7). Holders of renewable asylum-seeker permits were allowed to remain legally in South Africa until their claims were adjudicated. The mounting pressures on the refugee determination system and the costly failure of the deportation campaign led the South African government to introduce a moratorium on deportations that lasted from 2009 to 2012. It also implemented an "immigration amnesty" for Zimbabweans in 2010.[78] By the time the amnesty ended in mid-2011, a total of 242,371 Zimbabweans had been granted four-year residence permits in South Africa. In August 2014, the South African government introduced a new programme extending these permits by a further three years.

| Table 4: Deportations of Zimbabweans from South Africa, 1999-2008 | | | |
|---|---|---|---|
| | Deportations | | |
| | Total deportees | Zimbabwean deportees | Zimbabwean deportees as % of total |
| 1999 | 183,861 | 42,769 | 23.3 |
| 2000 | 145,575 | 45,922 | 31.5 |
| 2001 | 156,123 | 47,697 | 30.6 |
| 2002 | 135,870 | 38,118 | 28.1 |
| 2003 | 164,808 | 55,753 | 33.8 |
| 2004 | 167,137 | 72,112 | 43.1 |
| 2005 | 209,988 | 97,433 | 46.4 |
| 2006 | 266,067 | 109,532 | 41.2 |
| 2007 | 312,733 | 204,827 | 65.5 |
| 2008 | 280,837 | 164,678 | 58.6 |
| Source: Department of Home Affairs (South Africa) Annual Reports | | | |

A 2010 SAMP survey of working-age Zimbabweans in two South African cities (Cape Town and Johannesburg) prior to the amnesty found that 52% held asylum-seeker permits, 19% held work permits and only 2% had acquired permanent residence.[79] Until recently, most migrants from Zimbabwe engaged in circular migration, spending only short periods in South Africa, returning home frequently and showing little inclination to remain in South Africa. The 2010 SAMP survey was limited to migrants who had gone to South Africa for the first time between 2005 and 2010 and painted a very different picture. South Africa is increasingly seen as a longer-term destination rather than a temporary place to earn quick money. Nearly half of the respondents said that they wanted to remain in South Africa "for a few years" and another 21% that they wanted to remain indefinitely or permanently. In other words, two-thirds of recent migrants viewed a long-term stay in South Africa as desirable and many are bringing their families with them.

**Figure 7: Asylum Applications by Zimbabweans in South Africa, 2001-2010**

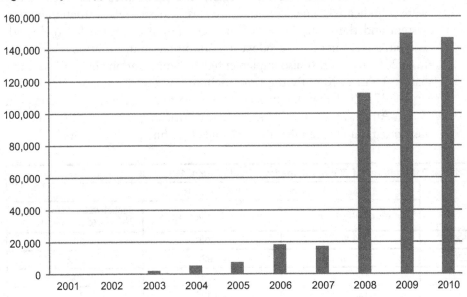

*Source: UNHCR Statistical Online Population Database*

Post-apartheid migration patterns between Mozambique and South Africa have a rather different history. The dominant form of movement between the two countries for most of the twentieth century was contract migration to the South African mines, predominantly from rural areas of Mozambique.[80] In the 1980s, however, the civil war in Mozambique led to a major influx of asylum-seekers, estimated to be anywhere between 300,000 and 400,000 people. Most settled along the border between the two countries and were integrated into local communities and worked on local farms.[81] Those who migrated to the cities tended to work in the informal economy although many were arrested and deported, with the number of deportations peaking at 156,000 in 1996 (Table 5). In 2000, an immigration amnesty gave South African residency status to an estimated 110,000 former refugees and the number of deportations immediately fell by 50%.[82] After 2004, and the abandonment of visa restrictions on Mozambicans, cross-border traffic increased from around 400,000 documented entries per annum to nearly 1.8 million in 2013 (Figure 8). As with Zimbabweans, the Mozambicans comprised a wide variety of migrants with different reasons for entry. And as with Zimbabweans, many of the migrants overstayed as "undocumented migrants" where they did menial jobs and worked in the informal economy.[83] However, one of the primary motivators was cross-border informal trade between Maputo and South African border towns as well as cities such as Johannesburg.

| Table 5: Deportation of Mozambicans from South Africa, 1990-2004 | | | |
|------|------|------|------|
| | Deportations | | |
| | Total deportees | Mozambican deportees | Mozambican deportees as % of total |
| 1990 | 53,418 | 42,330 | 79.2 |
| 1991 | 61,345 | 47,074 | 76.7 |
| 1992 | 82,575 | 61,210 | 74.1 |
| 1993 | 96,600 | 80,926 | 83.8 |
| 1994 | 90,692 | 74,279 | 81.9 |
| 1995 | 157,084 | 131,689 | 83.8 |
| 1996 | 180,713 | 157,425 | 87.1 |
| 1997 | 176,351 | 146,285 | 83.0 |
| 1998 | 181,286 | 141,506 | 78.1 |
| 1999 | 183,861 | 123,961 | 67.4 |
| 2000 | 145,575 | 84,738 | 58.2 |
| 2001 | 156,123 | 94,404 | 60.5 |
| 2002 | 151,653 | 83,695 | 55.2 |
| 2003 | 164,808 | 82,067 | 49.8 |
| 2004 | 167,137 | 81,619 | 48.8 |
| Note: Deportation figures for Mozambique are available only up to 2004 | | | |
| Source: Department of Home Affairs (South Africa) Annual Reports | | | |

**Figure 8: Legal Entries of Mozambicans into South Africa, 1999-2013**

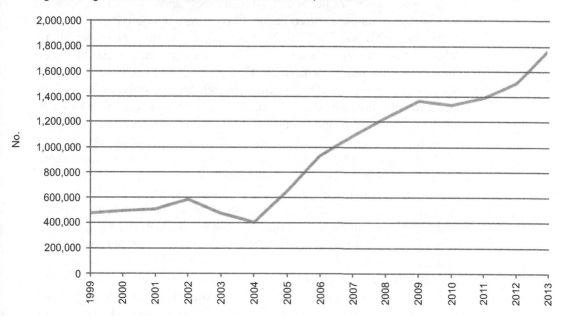

Source: Statistics South Africa, Various Reports

## MIGRANTS AND THE INFORMAL ECONOMY

Mobility is essential to the operation and dynamism of the urban informal economy in Southern African cities. Within urban areas, mobility is a vital component of the business strategies of informal operatives who identify spaces with niche markets or a relative absence of the formal sector. While some businesses operate from fixed sites others are extremely mobile, operating in different parts of the city on different days or at different times of a single day. Many of the participants in the informal economy are internal or international migrants, often in competition with one another for the same market share. Although the numbers of international migrants are frequently exaggerated, it is clear that they have played an increasingly important role in the informal economies of Southern African cities over the last two decades and have reshaped the nature of informality and informal entrepreneurship in the region. Yet the importance of that role is often underestimated, invisible to researchers and denigrated by policy-makers.[84]

The emerging literature on migrant entrepreneurship in South Africa focuses on several issues:

- Migration histories and the demographic profile of migrant entrepreneurs;[85]
- The activities and business strategies of migrant entrepreneurs;[86]
- The ethnic networks that enable access to resources such as business capital, cost-saving strategies such as shared shop spaces, revenue-boosting strategies such as bulk buying, and material support such as accommodation for newly-arrived migrants;[87] and
- The role of migrant entrepreneurs in creating employment.

In the 1990s and early 2000s, most migrant entrepreneurs settled in Johannesburg or Cape Town.[88] These two cities continue to be the major sites of informal migrant enterprise. However, one of the distinctive spatial features of migrant entrepreneurship is its diffusion throughout the country and down the urban hierarchy to many intermediate and smaller cities. A growing number of recent studies attest to the increase in business activity of migrant entrepreneurs in other South African urban centres.[89] This is a response to the fact that the policing of informality and immigration is more relaxed in smaller centres, as well as being a search for new markets.

According to census data, rates of unemployment amongst migrants in South Africa are generally lower than amongst South Africans, varying from a low of 6% in the case of Indian migrants to a high of 30% in the case of migrants from Lesotho. Only 18% of Zimbabwean and 24% of Mozambican migrants were unemployed in 2011 (Table 3). Many of those formally recorded as unemployed are, in fact, working in the informal economy.[90] A 2010 SAMP survey of post-2005 Zimbabwean migrants in Johannesburg and Cape Town, for example, found that 20% were involved in the informal economy.[91] Studies of other migrant groups such as Somalis suggest even higher rates of informal economy participation.[92] Asylum seekers and refugees from various countries are largely excluded from the formal labour market and show high levels of enterprise and innovation in the informal economy.[93]

The Bureau of Market Research estimated that 80% of 4,584 informal traders in inner-city Johannesburg in 2004 were non-South Africans, with 30% Nigerians, 30% Ethiopians and Somalis and 20% a mixture of Rwandans, Congolese and Zimbabweans.[94] A recent analysis of the 2012 South African Quarterly Labour Force Survey (Q3) showed clear differences between South Africans and international migrants.[95] For example, 21% of international migrants were classified as self-employed compared with 7% of internal migrants and 9% of non-migrants. However, only 13% of the total number of self-employed were international migrants compared with 15% of internal migrants and 71% of non-migrants. These differences were amplified in data by sector. As many as 33% of international migrants were in the informal sector, compared with 11% of internal migrants and 16% of non-migrants. Again, the absolute number of international migrants was much smaller, at 12% of the total compared with 14% of internal migrants and 74% of non-migrants. There is also evidence of a growing diversification of migrant source countries. Most migrants are still from neighbouring countries but there are growing numbers from many other African countries as well as farther afield, including Bangladesh, Pakistan and China.[96]

Migrants are often more entrepreneurial than most, yet the constraints they face in establishing and growing their businesses are considerable. Their general contribution to employment creation and inclusive growth is undervalued and often misrepresented as a threat. Foreign migrants in the South African informal economy do have considerable entrepreneurial ambition but are severely hampered in growing their enterprises by a range of obstacles.[97] These have not been systematically researched but include:

- National immigration and refugee policies, which determine the terms and conditions of entry and the ability to move along migration corridors between countries;
- Documentation, which determines the degree of access to social, financial and support services;
- Immigration law enforcement, with the ever-present threat of arrest and deportation disrupting business activity;
- Lack of access to credit (refugees and asylum seekers are commonly refused bank accounts and loans);
- Municipal regulations, which are generally unfriendly to the informal sector; and
- Hostile and xenophobic local attitudes.[98]

Violent attacks on the persons and properties of migrant business operations – whether motivated by rivalry, criminality or xenophobia or a combination of these – are regular and frequent and involve considerable loss of life. The nature and challenges posed by violence against migrant entrepreneurs are considered in detail in two companion SAMP reports.[99]

In terms of economic challenges confronting informal-sector entrepreneurs, both South African and migrant, a major issue is the lack of access to financial services including start-up capital and ongoing credit. Formal financial institutions are extremely reluctant to do business with migrant informal entrepreneurs. These entrepreneurs "have limited access to debt finance from commercial banks as they have problems in opening bank accounts, and acquiring visas and permits. In addition, most…have never applied for credit, despite the need for credit and may thus be classified as discouraged borrowers."[100] Fatoki's study of 148 migrant entrepreneurs in inner-city Johannesburg found that 29% had applied for credit and another 43% who were in need of credit had not. Of those who applied, only a third were successful.[101] Tengeh's study of 135 migrant entrepreneurs in Cape Town found that only 10% had obtained a bank loan to start their businesses.[102] Khosa's recent study of 93 Cape Town entrepreneurs from 19 African countries found that only 9% had acquired a bank loan as start-up capital compared with 37% who had used personal funds and 36% who had relied on family and friends.[103] As a result of the lack of credit, many migrant entrepreneurs rely on various financial bootstrapping alternatives to minimize their capital outlay and running costs (Table 6).

Despite these financial challenges, there is evidence of upward mobility of migrant-owned businesses in terms of the growth of business capital. In one study, the majority of African immigrant entrepreneurs in Cape Town (71%) had initial start-up business capital in the ZAR1,000 to ZAR5,000 range. After three or more years of operation the financial capital of nearly 40% had grown to an estimated range of ZAR50,000 to ZAR100,000.[105] This was a notable achievement in an environment where the rate of new-business failure is estimated at between 70% and 80%.[106] Immigrant entrepreneurs in South Africa, for instance, have long working hours, resulting in increased gross earnings.[107] Through risk-taking and heavy investment in their businesses, some entrepreneurs have been able to increase the size of their operations and have even managed to turn them into formal businesses.[108] Many use mobile phones and other technology that allows for increased interaction with suppliers and customers while reducing the need to travel.[109] Some also make use of social media, for instance, advertising their services on Facebook. However, a large number still lack access to computers, and records continue to be kept manually.[110] It has been suggested that the success of some immigrant-owned businesses in South Africa is largely due to immigrant entrepreneurs' superior qualifications. One study in Cape Town, for example, showed that at least 30% had completed tertiary education.[111] Empirically, it has been demonstrated that learning contributes to higher levels of earnings by providing a solid basis for the development of an entrepreneurial culture.[112]

| Table 6: Financial Bootstrapping by Migrant Entrepreneurs in Inner-City Johannesburg | | |
|---|---|---|
| | No. | % |
| Share premises with others | 141 | 95 |
| Delay owner's/manager's salary | 136 | 92 |
| Obtain loans from family and friends | 123 | 83 |
| Employ relatives and/or friends at non-market salary | 115 | 78 |
| Seek out best conditions possible with suppliers | 113 | 76 |
| Buy on consignment from suppliers | 108 | 73 |
| Contribute capital via other projects that pay the owner | 101 | 68 |
| Offer customers discounts for cash payments | 86 | 58 |
| Get payments in advance from customers | 80 | 54 |
| Use manager's private credit card for business expenses | 77 | 52 |
| Buy used rather than new equipment | 77 | 52 |
| Deliberately delay payments to suppliers | 76 | 51 |
| Deliberately choose customers who pay quickly | 73 | 49 |
| End a business relationship with a frequently-late-paying customer | 72 | 48 |
| Use different routines for minimizing capital invested in stock | 65 | 44 |
| Use routines to speed up invoicing | 62 | 42 |
| Coordinate purchases with other businesses (for better agreements) | 61 | 41 |
| Borrow equipment or machinery from other businesses | 56 | 38 |
| Hire staff for short periods instead of employing permanently | 56 | 38 |
| Share equipment with other businesses | 37 | 25 |
| Give the same terms of payment to all customers | 16 | 11 |
| Source: Fatoki[104] | | |

Proponents of the idea of "brain waste" argue that the educational qualifications of migrants are devalued and wasted if they cannot obtain suitable employment in the formal economy. This may well be the case when migrants are unable to obtain jobs that are commensurate with their levels of education and training. However, the brain-waste thesis also suggests that working in the informal economy is the ultimate form of wastage, "where educated immigrants find employment in the informal sector, which is typically characterised by low worker productivity, poor working conditions, low or non-existent worker protection and uncertain job prospects."[113] While this is not necessarily incorrect regarding employment in the informal economy, it ignores the fact that many educated migrant entrepreneurs are business owners employing others. Formal qualifications and experience might not have prepared them for running an informal business but these are not necessarily wasted if used to make a success of a new enterprise.

A central premise of the hostility towards foreign migrants in South Africa is that they "steal" jobs from South Africans. However, a study in Johannesburg in the late 1990s suggested that migrant-owned businesses actually created jobs for South Africans through direct hire.[114] This finding has been widely cited and generalized but was based on a small sample in a localized area of the city so its representativeness is unknown. Subsequent case study research has consistently corroborated that migrant entrepreneurs generate employment for other migrants and for South Africans.[115] Tengeh's study of 135 migrant entrepreneurs from Cameroon, Ethiopia, Ghana, Senegal and Somalia in Cape Town, for example, found that 70 (52%) had paid employees. Of these, 48% employed South Africans and 52% employed family members or members of the same ethnic group.[116] As many as 70% agreed or strongly agreed that when they started their businesses, most of their employees were South Africans. However, as their businesses grew, they tended to employ more people from their home country.[117]

Kalitanyi's study of 120 migrant entrepreneurs from Somalia, Nigeria and Senegal, also in Cape Town, found that 82% employed South Africans, 4% employed non-South Africans and 14% employed both.[118] Although the majority in all three groups preferred to hire South Africans, the preference was strongest amongst Senegalese and weakest amongst Nigerians. Seventy-four percent of the entrepreneurs said that they had transferred skills to South Africans in the process of employing them. More research is needed, however, on why migrant entrepreneurs employ South Africans and under what conditions. The essence of an inclusive growth perspective on informality is that the sector should create "decent jobs". Whether or not the jobs created deserve this label has yet to be established.

A different picture emerges in Radipere's comparative study of 220 South African-owned and 214 migrant-owned SMMEs in Tshwane and Johannesburg.[119] Two-thirds of the South African enterprises employed other South Africans and only 5% employed non-South Africans (Table 7). Nearly 30% employed both. Only 12% of the migrant-owned enterprises employed only South Africans while 40% employed only other migrants. The largest number, almost half, employed South Africans and non-South Africans. Since the three studies all tended to focus on similar sectors, it is possible that the employment practices vary between Gauteng and Cape Town.

| Table 7: Employment Creation by Informal Entrepreneurs, Tshwane and Johannesburg | | |
|---|---|---|
| | South African-owned (%) | Foreign-owned (%) |
| South African employees | 64.8 | 11.8 |
| Foreign employees | 4.7 | 39.6 |
| South African and foreign employees | 28.6 | 48.1 |
| Other employees | 1.9 | 0.5 |
| N | 220 | 214 |
| Source: Radipere[120] | | |

## INFORMAL CROSS-BORDER TRADING

Since the end of apartheid, South Africa has emerged as a market and source of goods for small-scale entrepreneurs whose short-term temporary visits are often conducted under the legal umbrella of visiting or tourism.[121] When it comes to relations between South Africa, Mozambique and Zimbabwe, most of this business is conducted by individuals travelling overland and engaged in so-called ICBT (informal cross-border trade). ICBT is a major catalyst for involvement in informal economies globally.[122] Trading across borders plays a vital, though largely unrecognized, role in regional economic integration and in linking informal economies in different SADC cities. This requires a perspective on informality that takes into account the impacts of interaction between different urban informal spaces across the region.[123] The volume of cross-border trade has been monitored at border control points in previous studies and there is a need to update and compare the current situation with that in the past and assess whether changes in the immigration regimes of the region, and the growth of informality in cities, have impacted on the volume of trade and the types of goods being transported.[124] More than that, informal traders need to be seen as entrepreneurs per se and their activities as a potentially strong promoter of inclusive growth and employment creation across the region. There has certainly been a tendency in the past to view informal traders as sole operators rather than micro-enterprises with the potential to grow significantly, to create jobs and to generate the capital to branch out into other sectors of the informal and formal economy.

In Mozambique and Zimbabwe, a sizeable number of informal entrepreneurs are international migrants. They establish their businesses in their home cities such as Harare and Maputo and grow them by taking advantage of the opportunities provided by cross-border economic linkages and migration. Informal cross-border traders, many of them women, thus play a critical role in the circulation of formally and informally produced goods throughout the SADC region.[125] The African Development Bank estimates that informal cross-border trade constitutes between 30% and 40% of total intra-SADC trade with an average annual value of USD17.6 billion.[126] There have been some efforts to monitor the overall volume of trade in foodstuffs, most notably by FEWSNET.[127] There are marked annual fluctuations in informal flows of maize, rice and beans depending on domestic harvests and market opportunities (Figure 9).

**Figure 9: Intra-SADC Informal Cross-Border Trade in Food Staples, 2005-2012**

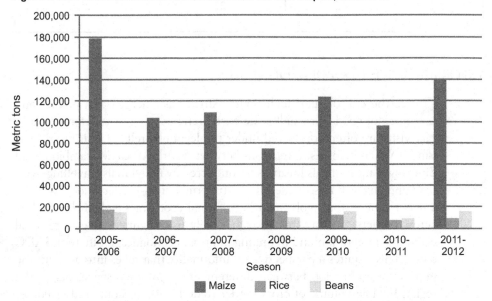

Source: FEWSNET[128]

A SAMP border-monitoring survey of 85,000 traders found that some crossed borders to buy goods for sale in their home countries (53% of the total), some took goods to sell in another country (32%) and some bought and sold in countries of origin and destination as "two-way" traders (13%) (Table 8).[129] The relative importance of these three trading types varied from country to country. In the case of Mozambique, the vast majority of traders go to buy goods, mainly in South Africa, for sale at home (81%) and very few (1%) take goods from Mozambique to sell. By contrast, only 27% of traders from Zimbabwe go to buy goods to bring home and 21% take goods from Zimbabwe to sell. Two-way trading is the most important form of activity in Zimbabwe (with 48% compared to only 12% of Mozambican traders). The survey also examined the types of goods being carried across borders. A wide variety of goods was being brought back to sell in the home country although, again, there was considerable inter-country variation (Table 9). Food items (processed and fresh) were clearly the most important but there was also considerable trade in new and second-hand clothing and household goods. The differences between Zimbabwe and Mozambique were, however, relatively slight with similar proportions of traders carrying groceries and clothing. The only significant difference was with fresh produce, which was more likely to be carried to Mozambique than Zimbabwe.

| Table 8: Type of Cross-Border Trading Activity (%) | | | | |
|---|---|---|---|---|
| Country of survey | One-way traders | | Two-way traders | Other |
| | Bringing back goods to sell | Taking goods to sell | | |
| Botswana | 25 | 66 | 7 | 2 |
| Lesotho | 81 | 19 | 0 | 0 |
| Malawi | 60 | 37 | 3 | 0 |
| Mozambique | 81 | 1 | 12 | 6 |
| Namibia | 54 | 44 | 1 | 0 |
| Swaziland | 88 | 8 | 1 | 2 |
| Zambia | 58 | 37 | 5 | 1 |
| Zimbabwe | 27 | 21 | 48 | 4 |
| Total | 53 | 32 | 13 | 2 |
| Source: SAMP[130] | | | | |

| Table 9: Types of Goods Carried by Cross-Border Traders for Sale in Home Country (%) | | | | | | | | | |
|---|---|---|---|---|---|---|---|---|---|
| Country of destination | Groceries | Fresh fruit & vegetables | Meat/ fish/ eggs | Electrical goods | Furniture | Household goods | Clothing/ shoes | Handicrafts/ curios | Other |
| Botswana | 8 | 27 | 1 | 1 | 1 | 16 | 19 | 10 | 21 |
| Lesotho | 10 | 31 | 1 | - | - | 6 | 17 | 10 | 24 |
| Malawi | 18 | 7 | 0 | 20 | 1 | 23 | 38 | 0 | 24 |
| Mozambique | 70 | 21 | 61 | 6 | 1 | 4 | 13 | - | 9 |
| Namibia | 56 | 16 | 6 | 3 | 1 | 8 | 3 | 2 | 19 |
| Swaziland | 4 | 7 | 0 | 3 | 1 | 19 | 65 | 1 | 10 |
| Zambia | 29 | 14 | 8 | 4 | 1 | 8 | 38 | 3 | 16 |
| Zimbabwe | 69 | 2 | 1 | 8 | 1 | 3 | 12 | 0 | 3 |
| Source: SAMP[131] | | | | | | | | | |

A survey of 120 cross-border traders in Johannesburg (just over a quarter of whom were from Mozambique and Zimbabwe) reached interesting findings about trading frequency and the financial spend of traders buying goods in South Africa for resale.[132] Seventy-two percent of the respondents were buying in South Africa for resale in their home countries and 26% had brought goods to sell in South Africa. The spend per trip was very significant, and certainly belies the image of impoverished survivalists often attached to cross-border traders. Nearly half spent more than ZAR10,000 per trip and two-thirds spent more than ZAR6,000 per trip (Figure 10). However, this does not capture the total spend since the vast majority enter South Africa more than once during the course of the average year. Over 90% made trips to South Africa three or more times per year (Figure 11). The survey also provided preliminary evidence about the challenges experienced by cross-border traders, most of which were non-economic (Table 10). For example, 40% mentioned crime and theft as a problem, 24% mentioned xenophobic discrimination and 22% police harassment.

**Figure 10: Money Spent in South Africa Per Visit by Cross-Border Traders**

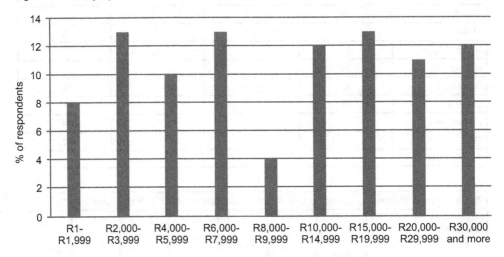

*Source: SPB[133]*

**Figure 11: Number of Trips to South Africa Per Year by Cross-Border Traders**

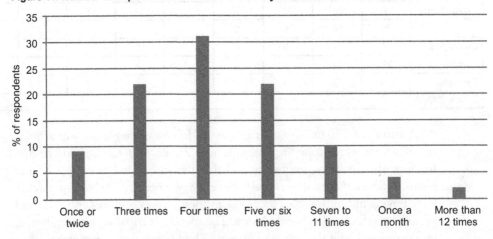

*Source: SPB[134]*

| Table 10: Problems Faced by Cross-Border Traders in Johannesburg | |
| --- | --- |
| Problem | % of respondents |
| Crime/theft | 39 |
| Cost/location/condition of accommodation | 29 |
| Discrimination/harassment due to xenophobia | 24 |
| Harassment by police | 23 |
| Visa, passport and trading licence application problems/time consumed | 22 |
| High rent of stalls | 15 |
| Transport problems | 11 |
| Tax and tax refund problems | 10 |
| Length of visa too short | 8 |
| Expensive items | 8 |
| Bad service from other stores and general public | 6 |
| Too few designated selling points | 6 |
| Border and customs control difficulties | 5 |
| Import duty procedures | 3 |
| Difficulties with securing work permits | 3 |
| Communication/language problems | 3 |
| Source: SPB[135] | |

In Harare, and other Zimbabwean cities, case-study research has been done on the profiles, activities, opportunities and obstacles that confront informal cross-border traders.[136] The literature on cross-border trading and the informal economy in Maputo is far more limited.[137] The primary focus of the Zimbabwean literature has been on informal cross-border trade as a survival and poverty alleviation strategy for women and their households in the face of severe economic crisis and unprecedented levels of formal unemployment. There is little evidence that cross-border trading represents an opportunity for sustained capital accumulation and business expansion for most. One of the reasons is the vulnerability of traders to exploitation and abuse during the course of their business activities. Crossing borders is itself a trial of demands for sex and bribes, eating into already small profits. Harassment en route and in cities of destination has forced traders to adopt strategies to protect themselves from criminality and xenophobic hostility.[138]

The literature on informal entrepreneurship tends to focus on the individual entrepreneur and firm rather than their forms of cooperation. Some cross-border traders in Zimbabwe have combined to form traders' associations to further their collective interests. For example, the Zimbabwe Cross Border Traders Association (ZCBTA) was formed in 2000 with a mandate "to promote and defend the interests of its members (and) to enhance the capacity of small scale traders/producers to create their own wealth through development of viable linkages and advocating for an enabling environment for the traders at all levels, i.e. nationally, regionally and globally."[139] It has just over 7,000 traders organized into trade committees and chapters across the country. ZCBTA and other trader organizations still only represent about 5%-7% of an estimated 300,000 cross-border traders. Their combined membership is three-quarters female. A more informal strategy of combination is a response to the dangers of travelling alone to South Africa to do business. Zimbabwean women travel together, reside with others and conduct their business in groups as a form of protection against the depredations of criminals and the police.[140]

## INFORMAL REMITTING ENTERPRISE

A related aspect of the relationship between migration and informal entrepreneurship is the massive flow of cash remittances and goods that migrants in Johannesburg and Cape Town send to Mozambique and Zimbabwe, including the cities of Maputo and Harare.[141] One study recently claimed that remittance flows from South Africa to other SADC countries increased from ZAR6.1 billion in 2006 to ZAR11.2 billion in 2012.[142] Although most migrants in South Africa tend to remit to rural households, there is evidence of a flow of remittances to households in both Maputo and Harare. The majority of remittances are sent to immediate or extended family members for their personal use. As a result, most remittances are spent on basic household needs including food, education, health and clothing. Only a very small proportion of remittances are saved or invested in productive enterprise. At the same time, the expenditure of remittances, especially on food and clothing, does benefit retailers in the informal economy of these cities. What we do not know is what proportion of remittances are generated within the informal economy of South Africa cities.

The business opportunities for small-scale entrepreneurs in the remittances industry relate more to the channels through which remittances of cash and goods are sent home by migrants. The use of formal remitting channels (banks and companies such as Western Union) for remittance transfers is very limited in both Mozambique and Zimbabwe. SAMP's 2006 Migration and Remittances Survey found that the vast majority of cash remittances are couriered by hand (personal or friends), by taxi drivers and by informal transport operators (Table 11).[143] Informal channels were clearly more important in Mozambique at that time, with 87% of migrants utilizing such channels to send remittances to their home country. Around half of Zimbabwean migrants used informal channels with a number preferring to use formal channels such as the post office (14.5%) and banks in Zimbabwe (23.5%). The subsequent economic collapse in Zimbabwe made it uneconomical for migrants to send money using formal channels. Money that was sent using formal channels was converted into Zimbabwean dollars at a rate fixed by the country's central bank, while the growing "black market" kept pace with the country's rapidly increasing inflation rate. This created a market for the entry of informal transport operators called the *Omalayisha* who operated largely from South Africa.[144] These informal entrepreneurs conducted their business in both directions, moving "cash, people – in good health, ill health or as corpses – consumer and material goods to Zimbabwe, and migrants to South Africa, a process that led to significant improvements in household food security and standards of living."[145]

| Table 11: Remittance Channels Used by Mozambican and Zimbabwean Migrants in South Africa | | |
|---|---|---|
| Remittance channel | Mozambique (%) | Zimbabwe (%) |
| Formal | | |
| Via post office | 0.8 | 14.5 |
| Spouse's TEBA account | 1.7 | 1.5 |
| Via bank in home country | 0.5 | 23.5 |
| Bank in South Africa | 0.2 | 1.3 |
| Via TEBA own account | 4.2 | 0.6 |
| Informal | | |
| Bring personally | 43.0 | 34.6 |
| Via friend/co-worker | 35.9 | 11.0 |
| Via taxis | 3.8 | 2.8 |
| Bus | 4.3 | 0.1 |
| Other method | 5.5 | 9.8 |
| Don't know | 0.0 | 0.2 |
| Source: Pendleton et al.[146] | | |

The remitting behaviour of informal sector mobile businesses and individuals is largely unknown, as is the role of remittances in building informal entrepreneurship in Harare and Maputo. Other key unanswered questions include: (a) how are the financial benefits of informal entrepreneurship distributed between South Africa (local spend), and Zimbabwe and Mozambique (remittances)? (b) do demands for remittances by households for living expenses in Zimbabwe and Mozambique reduce the inclination to grow and reinvest in South Africa? (c) could informal income in South Africa be used to provide start-up capital for enterprises in Harare and Maputo? and (d) how does informal remitting (which dominates the remitting behaviour of migrants in general) compare with formal remitting in terms of costs and benefits to informal economy entrepreneurs and micro-enterprises?

In the cases of Harare and Maputo, migrant entrepreneurs are primarily citizens who use temporary migration to South Africa as a strategy to support their businesses in Zimbabwe and Mozambique. There are comparatively few foreign migrant entrepreneurs in these two cities. In South Africa, on the other hand, most migrant entrepreneurs are not citizens at all but come from other African countries. The key question, then, is whether and to what extent citizenship and its entitlements impact upon opportunities and strategies for growing an informal enterprise. A third possibility, about which little is known, is whether informal entrepreneurs operate businesses that straddle two or more cities. Given the high levels of mobility between Mozambique and Zimbabwe and South Africa this does seem likely. Particular attention needs to be given to straddling as a migrant business strategy.

## GENDER, MOBILITY AND ENTREPRENEURSHIP

Gender issues are of particular relevance to understanding the nature of informal enterprise in Southern African cities. Firstly, cross-border migration has always been highly gendered in Southern Africa. For decades, migration to South Africa from the rest of Africa was primarily the preserve of young men. As recently as 2006, the overall gender breakdown of SADC migrants was 86% male and 14% female.[147] However, a process of feminization of migration is under way with the numbers and proportion of female migrants to South Africa increasing rapidly.[148] This process has proceeded furthest in the case of Zimbabwe, where in 2006 as many as 44% of migrants were women. Many migrant women are either spouses of male migrants or heads of households. One reason for the feminization of migration is changing gender roles within countries of origin especially where traditional employers of male migrants, such as the South African mining industry, have gone into decline. This has forced more women into cross-border migration to South Africa where they can access low-wage employment.

Second, migrant women experience severe discrimination in urban labour markets. Formal sector employment is difficult to obtain, even for those with skills and education. Few economic sectors prefer to hire women over men – domestic service is one, commercial agriculture another. Working conditions in both are poor with few rights and high levels of exploitation. Unable to obtain work permits, many women are hired as irregular migrants, which heightens their vulnerability as they are deprived of legal recourse when wages are unpaid or they are abused in the workplace. The majority cannot obtain formal sector jobs at all and are forced into survivalist activities in the urban informal economy. The informal economy, particularly street trading, is dominated by women as a result.[149]

Third, in both Harare and Maputo, gender is a particularly significant axis of differentiation and opportunity within the informal economy. In the Harare of the 1990s, the majority of informal operations were owned and run by women.[150] The collapse of the formal economy pushed many more men into the sector and made the highly competitive informal business environment a site of new conflict.[151] Similar gender-based tussles have emerged within the informal economy of Maputo.[152] Cross-border trade between Zimbabwe, Mozambique and South Africa was initially dominated by women who were precluded from formal sector labour markets and used the proceeds to sustain their households, independent of male household heads.[153] In the last decade, higher rates of unemployment amongst men have prompted them to move into the trade, leading to growing gender conflict over control of sectors of the trade as well as the disposition of the proceeds of trade.

Fourth, migrant women face considerable challenges to entrepreneurship and building successful enterprises.[154] Some are internal and others external to the household. Patriarchal domination in the household is often an obstacle to innovation, independent activity and control over the proceeds of work. In addition, domestic responsibilities and entrenched gender roles deprive women of the time, resources and energy to devote to revenue-generating economic activity. Outside the household, women face exclusion as migrants and from the resources needed to grow an informal business successfully. On the other hand, migration can provide opportunity, freeing women from the constraints of patriarchy and facilitating empowerment through independent economic activity outside the direct control of male household members.[155]

Finally, supposedly gender-neutral migration policies have been shown to contain discriminatory provisions that penalize, and often criminalize, the mobility and livelihood strategies of marginalized migrant women. This has been particularly evident in the formulation and implementation of national immigration policy.[156] At the local level, municipal regulations and policing of the informal economy impact most directly and negatively on female entrepreneurs and traders who dominate this activity.[157] What is less clear is how municipal policies towards informal entrepreneurship enable or constrain the ability of women to grow their businesses and contribute to gender-sensitive inclusive growth. Women also face other non-economic obstacles in the form of parasitical male police and customs officials who control the corridors of movement.[158]

These gender-based issues can be reformulated as a set of key research questions: (a) does the feminization of migration impact on the nature of participation of women in the informal economy, are there gender differences in the types and opportunities for involvement of men and women in informal entrepreneurship and does small business development offer women (and especially women-headed households) a way out of urban poverty? (b) what kinds of gender-based challenges affect migrant female and not male entrepreneurs and what strategies do they adopt to establish and grow their businesses? (c) how do intra-household gender roles and expectations impact on the ability of women to establish and grow their informal enterprises? and (d) are national and local policies on migration and the informal economy disadvantageous to female entrepreneurs and what kinds of policy reforms would mitigate this situation?

## MIGRANT ENTREPRENEURIAL MOTIVATION

Researchers in other parts of the world have increasingly sought to document and understand the diverse motivations for informal entrepreneurship.[159] A common, if simplistic, distinction is often made between survivalist or marginalist or involuntary participants in the informal economy and those who choose informal over formal work because of the opportunities it provides. These two groups are often referred to as necessity-driven and opportunity-driven entrepreneurs.[160] The former have been described as follows: "their contribution is negligible and expected returns are low and intermittent, moreover they display low expectations of growth and job creation, and their motivation is all about personal survival."[161] In Southern Africa, until recently, attention tended to focus more on the survivalist activities and income-generating strategies of those in the informal economy. The underlying premise was that individuals in the informal sector were struggling to earn a living in conditions of extreme difficulty and marginalization. However, the "marginalization thesis" has been tested and found wanting in other contexts in Africa and there is no reason why it should be uncritically applied to South Africa, Mozambique and Zimbabwe.[162]

Participation in the informal economy may be enforced, in the sense that there are no alternatives, but that does not mean that all participants are therefore just "getting by" until a better opportunity presents itself in the formal economy. One psychological study of "necessity entrepreneurs" in Johannesburg, for example, found that they displayed "cognitive styles matching enterprising attitudes."[163] There is also considerable variability amongst so-called survivalists. A three-year study of street traders in inner-city Johannesburg, for example, found considerable variation in levels of satisfaction and a very strong statistical relationship between "continuance satisfaction" and levels of income.[164] The same research also found considerable variation in the psychological value systems of individual traders.[165]

One of the most vexing questions for small business advocates in South Africa is what is commonly seen as an underdeveloped entrepreneurial motivation or "spirit" amongst those living in more disadvantaged areas of the country.[166] Some studies have contested this stereotype while others have sought explanations that are lodged in the repressive legacy of apartheid and the dysfunctional South African education system.[167] The issue has been brought into sharp relief by South Africa's poor ranking in global entrepreneurship surveys and the relatively small size of the informal economy.[168] The perception that migrants are far more successful entrepreneurs than South Africans in the informal economy has prompted a new research focus on migrant entrepreneurial orientation and motivation and, by extension, comparisons with South African entrepreneurs.[169] One study of 500 SMMEs in the retail sector in Gauteng, however, found no significant difference between South Africans and migrants in terms of their motivation to start a business.[170] Another study of the entrepreneurial orientation of 339 South African (44%) and non-South African (56%) street traders in inner-city Johannesburg found, to the obvious surprise of the authors, that South Africans were more innovative than international migrants (with migrants to Johannesburg from other parts of South Africa the most innovative of all).[171] However, South Africans were associated with lower levels of the entrepreneurial qualities of "proactiveness" and "competitive aggression" and, overall, South African nationality was "negatively and significantly associated with total entrepreneurial orientation."[172] Competitive aggressiveness was also positively correlated with years spent in the city, days worked per week, and degree of training.[173] A third study focused on the spaza shop sector in Khayelitsha, Cape Town.[174] Of a total of 352 spaza owners interviewed, 214 (61%) were South Africans and 138 (39%) were international migrants. In both groups, the gender split was around 60% male and 40% female. Migrants scored better than South Africans on four separate indicators of entrepreneurial orientation: achievement, innovation, personal initiative and autonomy.

Other aspects of migrant entrepreneurial motivation have been examined in other case studies based on research in inner-city Johannesburg. Fatoki, for example, analysed the "competitive intelligence" of migrant-owned businesses in Johannesburg and found that competition information-seeking is performed by the majority of owners and their employees, especially to monitor the prices of their competitors.[175] This enables them to undercut their competition and attract more customers. The study also examined the growth expectations of migrant entrepreneurs and found a high degree of optimism.[176] Education, managerial experience, related experience, motivation and networking were all significant predictors of positive growth expectations. At the firm level, innovation and adequate access to finance were significant predictors of growth expectations.

## PATHOLOGIZING SPACE, POLICING INFORMALITY

The three countries (and four municipalities) discussed in this paper represent contrasting policy responses to the informal economy and informal migrant entrepreneurship. The predominant attitude towards the informal economy in Zimbabwe and Harare over the last decade has been extremely negative and repressive underwritten by a modernist view of city planning and the pathologizing of informal urban space, which are totally at odds with the reality of survival in a rapidly shrinking formal economy and mass unemployment.[177] These views culminated in the nationwide assault on informality by the Mugabe government through Operation Murambatsvina (Clean Out the Trash) in 2005, which attempted to destroy all manifestations of urban informality: businesses, markets and shelter.[178] The UN Habitat mission to Zimbabwe estimated that some 700,000 people in cities across the country lost either their homes, their source of livelihood or both.[179] Sites where informal economy workers gathered to market their wares, as well as formal markets, some of which had been in operation for decades, were targeted. An estimated 75,000 vendors in Harare alone were unable to work from late May, 2005.[180] The informal economy in cities like Harare was, in fact, a consequence of government policies and, in particular, the country's growing economic crisis.[181] With the collapse of the manufacturing base and commercial food production, the shelves in formal retail outlets emptied, providing new opportunities for informal entrepreneurship. Many moved to South Africa and countries overseas to procure goods unavailable locally for resale and opened up new markets for products made in Zimbabwe, particularly in the handicraft industry.

Operation Murambatsvina temporarily devastated the informal economy and the livelihoods of the urban poor in many Zimbabwean cities.[182] However, this reactionary and retrograde policy appears to have been no more than a temporary "fix" for its architects as informality quickly rebounded and returned to the urban spaces from which it had been erased.[183] The key policy question in Zimbabwe is what the impact of the official harassment has been on informal entrepreneurship and how informal entrepreneurs have responded to this policy through strategies of avoidance, resistance and flight. If Zimbabwe's economic recovery gathers pace, it is important to know whether the state will adopt a more tolerant approach to informality or whether the vast informal economy will continue to "fly under the radar" and be the target of renewed repression.

In Mozambique, and Maputo in particular, the national and municipal authorities have traditionally adopted a tolerant approach to the informal economy, primarily because it provides a livelihood to so many and because of the social unrest likely to be generated by a Zimbabwe-style assault.[184] Maputo has experienced food and fuel riots in recent years and any activity that lowers the cost of food is unlikely to be tampered with. While the informal economy has been subject to periodic harassment, it is generally viewed within official circles as an important and sustainable source of livelihood for the urban poor. However, as one study points out, the state is "not universally tolerant of informal activities" and has "embraced a modernizing agenda, aimed at promoting formalization."[185] The policy aim is not to eliminate informality but to "discourage" illegality through registration and formalization. One mechanism has been the establishment of formal urban markets where vendors pay rent for stands. However, many of these stands remain unoccupied. As one commentator noted: "What they say in Maputo is that there are thousands of spaces available in the legal official municipal markets which are not being taken up. People don't do this because if they move into the markets they will have to pay taxes. All these people would prefer to sell their stuff on the pavements."[186]

In 2008, a simplified tax for small businesses was introduced, payable as a percentage of turnover or as a lump sum. Any company, individual trader or producer with a volume of business less than about USD100,000 per year could opt for this tax instead of paying income, corporation and value-added taxes. However, uptake has been low.[187] To date, informal entrepreneurs have been largely resistant to such efforts, which are viewed as a "money grab by the state."[188] The vast majority (80%) of firms in a 2005 survey had no kind of documentation and were officially illegal.[189] According to Byiers, "it is important to understand why greater formalization might be desirable. While the government tends to focus on raising revenues, where micro informal firms are concerned, the benefit from formalization is more likely to be the secondary effects of allowing enterprises to operate legitimately, and thus potentially raising their productivity and ability to integrate more deeply with the national economy."[190]

There is some evidence that former informal operators who have registered and paid licences and taxes are more productive than those who spend a great deal of effort evading the authorities, but the obstacles to formalization and why this might be avoided or resisted need further research, as do the implications of formalization. Mozambique now has one of the fastest growing formal economies in Africa and the streetscape of major cities such as Maputo is being transformed. Policy pressures to formalize the informal economy, a basic precept of the many international agencies and donors that advise and provide resources for urban infrastructure, are likely to intensify. Already one of Maputo's major informal markets, Xikhelene, has been "upgraded", which has forced vendors to rent new stands and eliminated all associated trading on the streets around the market.[191]

The South African response to informality lies somewhere between the Mozambican and Zimbabwean, but has been neither consistent nor coherent. Given the vigorous suppression of informality by the apartheid state, it was likely that the country's first democratic state would reinforce the new policies of tolerance that emerged in the late 1980s. At the national level, the post-apartheid state introduced a set of support programmes to assist entrepreneurship development and upgrading of the small, medium and microenterprise (SMME) economy. Rogerson's review of the impacts of the first 10 years of the post-apartheid government's SMME programmes concluded, however, that "existing government SMME programmes largely have been biased towards the groups of small and medium-sized enterprises and to a large extent have by-passed micro-enterprises and the informal economy."[192] A detailed review of the efficacy of the South African government support measures to the informal economy during the post-apartheid period concluded that they were "few and far between, patchy and incoherent, and largely ineffective."[193] Another study demonstrates this has particularly been true for female entrepreneurs.[194]

Although these evaluations need to be updated, there are indications that very small economic players in the informal economy "continue to fall through the gaps in government policy."[195] Two recent initiatives from the Department of Trade and Industry (DTI) illustrate the kinds of anti-foreign thinking that inform the national government's policy response. In mid-March 2013, the DTI launched the National Informal Business Uplift-ment Strategy (NIBUS), the first nationally-coordinated policy approach to dealing with the informal sector, which has led to the establishment of the Shared Economic Infrastructure Facility (SEIF) and the Informal Busi-ness Upliftment Facility (IBUF) tackling infrastructure and skills deficits respectively. SEIF provides funding for new, upgrades or maintenance of infrastructure that is shared by informal businesses. Funding is available to municipalities on a 50:50 cost-sharing grant basis to a maximum of ZAR2 million. IBUF focuses on skills development, promotional material, product improvement, technology support, equipment, and help with regis-tration. This is being piloted through the training of 1,000 informal traders in a partnership with the Wholesale and Retail Sector Education and Train-ing Authority. The stated target of business upliftment is entrepreneurial activity in the informal economy. This, combined with an emphasis on graduation to the formal economy, runs the risk of "picking the winners" and neglecting the majority. Policy at both national and local level needs to recognize the diverse nature of informal activity and the fact that these activities require support that is quite specific.

The final NIBUS document has yet to be released by the DTI. However, the first two drafts express clear anti-foreign sentiment. The March 2013 draft, for example, states that "there are no regulatory restrictions in con-trolling the influx of foreigners, especially Chinese and Pakistanians; and it seems there is no synergy between the DTI and Home Affairs in devising strategies and policies to control foreign business activities." The January 2014 draft adds that "this strategic pillar further attends to foreign trader challenge as there is evidence of violence and unhappiness of local com-munities with regard to the takeover of local business by foreign nationals. A number of foreign traders are also illegal in the country and some are involved in the sale of illegal goods."

The second development is the tabling in Parliament of the Licensing of Businesses Bill in 2013 by the DTI. The Bill specifies that any person involved in business activities – no matter how small – will be required to have a licence. Members of the South African Police Service, traffic officers and peace officers, amongst others, would be given powers to enforce com-pliance – to conduct inspections, question any person, remove any goods on the premises and confiscate them and close any premises pending further investigation. Those found in contravention of the Act, once convicted would be liable for a fine of an unspecified amount or imprisonment for up to 10 years.[196] The Bill is extremely punitive and would result in large-scale criminalization of current livelihood activities. It was withdrawn for revision after a chorus of protest from the private sector, non-governmental organizations, academics and the media.

The sections of the Bill referring to migrants are especially relevant. The Bill states that licences will be only be given to non-citizens who have first acquired a business permit under the Immigration Act or a refugee permit under the Refugee Act.[197] Business permits have to be applied for in the country of origin and are only granted if the applicant can demonstrate that he or she has ZAR2.5 million to invest in South Africa. Few, if any, cross-border traders and migrant entrepreneurs currently operating in the South African informal economy would qualify. The Bill also suggests that community-based organizations, non-governmental organizations and others will be given the job of working with the licensing authorities to police this. The implication here is that South Africans could assist the police in identifying and "rooting out" foreign traders. The xenophobic attacks of 2008 demonstrated that there are elements in many communities who need no encouragement to turn on their neighbours from other African countries.

This shows a strong anti-foreign sentiment within national government with a focus on those operating in the informal economy. The Deputy Trade and Industry Minister, for example, has stated that "the scourge of South Africans in townships selling and renting their businesses to foreigners unfortunately does not assist us as government in our efforts to support and grow these informal businesses…You still find many spaza shops with African names, but when you go in to buy you find your Mohammeds and most of them are not even registered."[198] Such sentiments are echoed within the ruling African National Congress (ANC). The ANC National Executive Committee stated just prior to the 2014 national elections that "arising from issues raised on our door to door election campaign…it was decided that an in-depth research be commissioned to look into the best way of dealing with jobs particularly that do not require high level of skills that get taken by foreign nationals, equally such an in-depth research should also look into small trading impact by foreign nationals. It was agreed that once the research has been completed and the report compiled, further discussion will be undertaken with a view to refine our immigration policy."[199]

At the local level, in both Cape Town and Johannesburg, there are contradictions between policy statements affirming the positive contribution of the informal economy and the actual implementation of policy. Consider, for example, a particularly visible element of the informal economy – street trading. Johannesburg's street trading policy states that "informal trading is a positive development in the micro business sector as it contributes to the creation of jobs and alleviation of poverty and has the potential to expand further the City's economic base."[200] Cape Town's policy advocates for a "thriving informal trading sector that is valued and integrated into the economic life, urban landscape and social activities within the City of Cape Town."[201]

Yet, in late 2013, the Johannesburg City Council violently removed and confiscated the inventory of an estimated 6,000 inner-city street traders, many of them migrants. A group of traders took the city to court and, in April 2014, the Constitutional Court ruled in their favour with Acting Chief Justice Moseneke stating that the so-called Operation Clean Sweep was an act of "humiliation and degradation" and that the attitude of the City "may well border on the cynical."[202] Street traders have returned to the streets but their future remains uncertain. The City has commissioned a project to consider alternatives while simultaneously pursuing the declaration of large inner city areas restricted and prohibited trade zones.[203] Wafer's detailed analysis shows how the city has long been ambivalent, if not actively hostile, to the informal economy.[204] Recent research on inner-city Cape Town suggests that there is less draconian but more systemic exclusion exemplified by the allocation of only 410 street-trading bays in the whole inner city.[205] There is evidence of ongoing harassment of traders throughout the city.[206] Although the policy environment differs in different parts of the city and between different segments within the informal economy, the modernist vision of the "world-class city" with its associated antipathy towards informality and the pathologizing of informal space and activity seems to predominate.

Some of the most dedicated, enterprising and successful entrepreneurs in the South African informal economy are migrants to the country. Under any other circumstances they would probably be lauded by government as exemplars of small-scale and micro entrepreneurship. However, the state (and many citizens) view their activities as highly undesirable simply because of their national origins. Harassment, extortion and bribery of officialdom are some of the daily costs of doing business in South Africa. Many entrepreneurs, especially in informal settlements and townships, face constant security threats and enjoy minimal protection from the police.[207] Informal cross-border traders face another set of obstacles.[208] These include harassment by police and border guards, demands for inflated customs duties, transportation problems for goods, personal safety and security, unfriendly municipal regulations, and the difficulties of accessing credit. As a result they are unable to utilize their entrepreneurial skills and experience and grow their businesses in optimal fashion.

# CONCLUSION

In a recent discussion of the relationship between inclusive growth and informality, Heintz defines inclusive growth as growth that occurs in a context in which employment opportunities expand and improve, poor households' access to these opportunities increases, and inequalities are decreased. He suggests a research agenda focused on four main issues:

- The causal linkages between economic growth, economic development and informality;
- The barriers to economic mobility faced by individuals and enterprises in the informal economy, such as economic risk, transitions into and out of informal employment, gender-based constraints, and enterprise upgrading;
- Linkages between the formal and informal institutions, enterprises and employment; and
- Informality and the quality of informal employment.

While there are several references to mobility in Heintz's discussion, this is generally confined to economic mobility and not spatial mobility and the interactions between the economic and the spatial. For all its relevance, therefore, his proposed agenda overlooks a central characteristic and determinant of informality – human mobility and migration – and the ways in which it complicates the relationship between inclusive growth and informality.

In an analysis of the relationship between migration and inclusive growth in India, IDRC's Arjan de Haan argues that migration and migrants are largely invisible in policy debates.[209] He draws a parallel between outdated conceptions of the informal economy and migration that see both as transitional, noting that "as within the concept of informal sector, so with migrants there is a risk that the assumption of transitional existence may hinder creative thinking about ways in which migrants can be supported." Arguing that a strong anti-migrant bias pervades policy discussions, de Haan states that "policy makers around the world tend to regard migrants as vagrants, and perceive migration as a threat to stability, to social order, and/ or to national or regional identity." In Southern Africa, global debates about the positive aspects of the relationship between migration and development have made limited headway.[210] Instead, migration is viewed by politicians and policy-makers alike as something to be resisted and controlled and migrants themselves as threats, parasites, job-stealers and law-breakers. The creative potential and possibilities of migrant entrepreneurship, whether survivalist or opportunistic, are ignored and regulatory barriers are constantly created and reinforced. Ironically, migrant entrepreneurs in South Africa from Zimbabwe, Mozambique and other African countries would be lauded as economic innovators and exemplars, but for the fact that they carry the labels "foreigner" and "outsider."

The backdrop for the Growing Informal Cities (GIC) Project's focus on informality and migrant entrepreneurship is regional integration, rapid urbanization and the expansion of informal urban economies in the Southern African cities of Cape Town, Johannesburg, Maputo and Harare. With high rates of formal unemployment in most countries, the informal economy has emerged as a major source of income and livelihoods for poor urban households. Migrants in and from all four cities play a critical role in the informal economy yet the importance of that role is often underestimated and invisible to researchers and policy-makers. Migrants may be more entrepreneurial than most, yet the constraints and obstacles they face in establishing and growing their businesses are massive. Their general contribution to employment creation and inclusive growth is undervalued and often misrepresented as a threat, they face particular difficulties in accessing microfinance and the formal banking system, they are often excluded from SMME training programmes and they frequently run afoul of badly-managed and often corrupt systems of immigration and border control.

The purpose of the GIC is to examine and profile the "hidden" role of migrant informal entrepreneurship in different Southern African cities. The cities were chosen for analysis and comparison because they represent different forms of migrant entrepreneurship. In South African cities like Cape Town and Johannesburg, migrant entrepreneurs come from throughout Africa including Zimbabwe and Mozambique. In Maputo and Harare, most migrant entrepreneurs are local but they structure their businesses around the opportunities afforded by growing regional integration and cross-border migration to and from South Africa. Policies towards informality and informal entrepreneurship vary from country to country. In Zimbabwe, the informal economy has been ruthlessly repressed but survives nonetheless. In Mozambique, there is a laissez-faire attitude towards the informal economy and attempts to formalize informal businesses through registration have not been particularly successful. In South Africa, informality is generally encouraged at the national level through training programmes and support activities. But at the municipal level, the informal economy is often viewed in negative terms and pathologized. The impacts of national and municipal programmes and actions are uncertain especially for migrant entrepreneurs. Indeed, these entrepreneurs, who could and do contribute to inclusive growth, are subjected to social and economic exclusion that spills over into xenophobia.

The GIC is generating a comparative body of knowledge about informal migrant entrepreneurs, raising their profile in regional, national and municipal policy debates with a view to effecting positive change in the regulatory environment in which they operate. By allowing migrant entrepreneurs to expand and reach their full potential, free of harassment and exclusion, a major contribution can be made to facilitating inclusive growth through informal entrepreneurship. To this end, GIC will advance understanding of the reciprocal links between mobility and informal entrepreneurship in Southern African cities through a programme of ongoing rigorous research oriented to the economic growth and poverty reduction goals of SADC governments, and impacting on policy implementation processes around migration, development and urban management. The more specific objectives of GIC are:

- Enhancing the evidence base on the links between migration and informalization in Southern African cities and examining the implications for municipal, national and regional immigration and urban development policy;
- Analyzing the role played by international migrants in the informal economy of particular cities (Cape Town and Johannesburg) and the role of cross-border migration in the informal economy of others (Harare and Maputo) and identifying the obstacles that migrant entrepreneurs face in maximizing the growth and employment creation potential of their businesses; and
- Developing a framework for facilitating greater opportunities for informal entrepreneurship amongst migrants, including refugees and female entrepreneurs.

In order to better understand the linkages between migration, informality and inclusive growth in Cape Town and Johannesburg , GIC is undertaking the following activities:

- A survey of a sample of 1,000 migrant-owned micro-enterprises in Cape Town and Johannesburg in various sectors of the informal economy. Information is being gathered on characteristics of the micro-enterprise (including origins, ownership, structure, capitalization) activities (with a particular emphasis on mobile marketing strategies), income generation, employment creation potential, entrepreneurial orientation and performance in the informal economy;
- In Gauteng, a complementary survey of 1,000 South-African-owned enterprises, which will allow for comparative analysis of the make-up and business strategies of South African versus migrant-owned enterprises in the informal economy;
- Qualitative interviews and focus groups with 100 migrant informal entrepreneurs to ascertain institutional and other problems faced in growing businesses; and
- Interviews with key informants in municipalities including business associations and policy-makers on attitudes towards regulation and support of migrant entrepreneurs.

The GIC is also focusing on informal cross-border traders who use migration as a strategy to sustain and grow their businesses. Research includes:

- A survey of 1,000 Mozambican and Zimbabwean informal traders in

Harare and Maputo for information on participants, economic activities, challenges, business strategies and migration behaviour;

- In-depth qualitative interviews with 100 Mozambican and Zimbabwean traders with a focus on migration-related strategies to build and grow informal businesses and attitudes towards policy regulation of their activities;
- A complementary survey of 500 cross-border traders in the city of Johannesburg; and
- Focus group interviews with national and municipal officials, formal sector businesses, unions and traders' associations on policy frameworks and impacts on migrant entrepreneurship.

Finally, the GIC is examining national and municipal regulatory frameworks around informality and informal entrepreneurship with a focus on the opportunities and obstacles that these frameworks pose to the establishment and growth of migrant businesses including:

- A comparative audit of national and municipal policies and regulations that affect informal migrant entrepreneurs in South Africa, Mozambique and Zimbabwe;
- An inventory of small-enterprise policies and strategies and assessment of whether migrants and refugees have access to these programmes; and
- Key informant interviews to ascertain perceived impacts of existing policies and potential impacts of policies that could be used to grow informal migrant businesses.

The results and policy implications of this programme of research will be published in forthcoming reports in this special SAMP series.

## ENDNOTES

1   *The State of the World Cities Report 2006-7* (Nairobi: UNHABITAT, 2007).

2   *The State of African Cities 2008: A Framework for Addressing Urban Challenges in Africa* (Nairobi: UNHABITAT, 2008).

3   *The State of African Cities 2014: Reimagining Sustainable Urban Transitions* (Nairobi: UNHABITAT, 2014).

4   E. Pieterse, *City Futures: Confronting the Crisis of Urban Development* (London: Zed Books, 2008); S. Parnell and E. Pieterse, eds., *Africa's Urban Revolution* (London: Zed Books, 2014).

5   UN Department of Economic and Social Affairs, Population Division, *World Urbanization Prospects: The 2014 Revision* (New York: United Nations, 2014).

6   Ibid.

7   K. Tranberg Hansen and M. Vaa, eds., *Reconsidering Informality: Perspectives from Urban Africa* (Uppsala, 2002); A. Simone, *For the City Yet to Come: Changing African Life in Four Cities* (Durham NC, 2004); A. Simone and A. Abouhani, eds., *Urban Africa: Changing Contours of Survival in the City* (London: Zed Books, 2005); D. Potts, "The Urban Informal Sector in Sub-Saharan Africa: From Bad to Good (and Back Again?)" *Development Southern Africa* 25(2008): 151-67; D. Sparks and S. Barnett, "The Informal Sector in Sub-Saharan Africa: Out of the Shadows to Foster Sustainable Employment and Equity?" *International Business & Economics Research Journal* 9(5) (2010).

8   A. Simone, "Africities: Popular Engagements of the Urban in Contemporary Africa" *Space and Culture* 4(2001): 252.

9   Economic Commission for Africa, "Chapter 5: Informal Trade in Africa" In *Assessing Regional Integration in Africa IV: Enhancing Intra-African Trade* (Addis Ababa, 2010), p. 143.

10  C. Kessides, "The Urban Transition in Sub-Saharan Africa: Implications for Economic Growth and Poverty Reduction" Africa Region Working Paper Series No. 97, World Bank, Washington DC, 2005.

11  D. Potts, "The State and the Informal in Sub-Saharan African Urban Economies: Revisiting Debates on Dualism" Crisis States Working Papers Series No. 2, London School of Economics, 2007.

12  The ILO and WIEGO use International Conference of Labour Statisticians definitions. Informal employment refers to all employment arrangements that do not provide individuals with legal or social protections through their work (regardless of whether the individual works in the formal or informal sector) while informal sector employment refers to employment that takes place in unincorporated small or unregistered enterprises (for example those having fewer than five employees); see ILO, *Women and Men in the Informal Economy: A Statistical Picture* (Geneva: ILO, 2013), pp. 2-3 for more details.

13  J. Vanek, M. Chen, F. Carré, J. Heintz and R. Hussmanns, "Statistics on the Informal Economy: Definitions, Regional Estimates and Challenges" Working

Paper (Statistics) No. 2, WIEGO, 2014, p. 1; and J. Charmes, "The Informal Economy Worldwide: Trends and Characteristics" *Margin: The Journal of Applied Economic Research* 6(2012): 103-132.

14  Adapted from ILO, "Women and Men in the Informal Economy" p. 10.

15  Ibid., p. 24.

16  Ibid., p. 21.

17  S. Peberdy and C. Rogerson, "Transnationalism and Non-South African Entrepreneurs in South Africa's Small, Medium and Micro-Enterprise (SMME) Economy" In J. Crush and D. McDonald, eds., *Transnationalism and New African Immigration to South Africa* (Toronto: CAAS, 2002), pp. 20-40; S. Peberdy and C. Rogerson, "South Africa: Creating New Spaces?" In R. Kloosterman and J. Rath, eds., *Immigrant Entrepreneurs: Venturing Abroad in the Age of Globalization* (Oxford: Berg, 2003), pp. 79-100; C. Skinner, "Street Trade in Africa: A Review" Working Paper No. 51, School of Development Studies, UKZN, Durban, 2008.

18  J. Crush, S. Ramachandran and W. Pendleton, *Soft Targets: Xenophobia, Public Violence and Changing Attitudes to Migrants in South Africa After May 2008*, SAMP Migration Policy Series No. 64, Cape Town, 2013.

19  A. Charman and L. Piper, "Xenophobia, Criminality and Violent Entrepreneurship: Violence against Somali Shopkeepers in Delft South, Cape Town, South Africa" *South African Review of Sociology* 43(2012): 81-105.

20  Statistics South Africa defines the informal sector as having the following two components: (a) employees working in establishments that employ fewer than five employees, who do not deduct income tax from their salaries/wages; and (b) employers, own-account workers and persons helping unpaid in their household business who are not registered for either income tax or value-added tax; Statistics South Africa, *Quarterly Labour Force Survey*, Quarter 2, 2014, Statistical Release P0211, p. v.

21  Ibid.

22  M. Rogan and C. Skinner, "Employment in the South African Informal Sector: Interrogating Trends; Identifying Opportunities" SALDRU Working Paper, UCT (forthcoming).

23  ILO, *Women and Men in the Informal Economy* (2013), p. 13.

24  Rogan and Skinner, "Employment in the South African Informal Sector."

25  A discouraged job-seeker is defined as a person who was not employed during the reference period, wanted to work, was available to work/start a business but did not take active steps to find work during the previous four weeks.

26  Own calculations using Statistics South Africa, *Quarterly Labour Force Survey*, Quarter 2, 2014, Statistical Release P0211, p. v.

27  C. Rogerson, "Late Apartheid and the Urban Informal Sector" In J. Suckling and L. White, eds., *After Apartheid: Renewal of the South African Economy* (London: James Currey, 1988), pp. 132-45.

28  P. Chicello, C. Almeleh, L. Mncube and M. Oosthuizen, "Perceived Barriers

to Entry into Self-Employment in Khayelitsha, South Africa: Crime, Risk and Start-Up Capital Dominate Profit Concerns" CSSR Working Paper No. 300, University of Cape Town, 2011; P. Cichello, L. Mncube, M. Oosthuizen and L. Poswell, "Economists versus the Street: Comparative Viewpoints on Barriers to Self-employment in Khayelitsha, South Africa" DPRU Working Paper No. 11/144, University of Cape Town, 2012.

29  Rogan and Skinner, "Employment in the South African Informal Sector."

30  Gauteng City-Region Observatory, "City Benchmarking: Quality of Life Survey 2013" (Johannesburg: Gauteng City-Region Observatory, 2014).

31  D. Woodward, R. Rolfe, A. Ligthelm and P. Guimarães, "The Viability of Informal Micro-Enterprise in South Africa" *Journal of Developmental Entrepreneurship* 16(2011): 65–86.

32  A. Ligthelm, "Survival Analysis of Small Informal Businesses in South Africa, 2007-2010" *Eurasian Business Review* 1(2011): 160-79.

33  A. Ligthelm."Measuring the Size of the Informal Economy in South Africa, 2004/05" Bureau of Market Research, Unisa, Pretoria, 2005.

34  A. Ligthelm, "Profile of Informal Microenterprises in the Retail Sector of South Africa" *Southern African Business Review* 8(2004): 39-52; J. Benekem M. Curran, G. Forsyth and S. Lamb, "Towards an Understanding of Retailing Practices in the Second Economy: An Exploratory Study of Western and Eastern Cape Township Retailers in South Africa" *African Journal of Business and Economic Research* 6(2011): 92-108; D. du Plessis, H. Geyer and A. van Eeden, "On the Role of the Informal Sector in the Changing Socio-Economic Landscape of the Cape Town Metropolitan Area" *Social Space* 1(2011): 1-20.

35  C. Callaghan, "Entrepreneurial Orientation and Entrepreneurial Performance of Central Johannesburg Informal Sector Street Traders" M. Comm. Thesis, University of the Witwatersrand, 2009; K. Tissington, "The Business of Survival: Informal Trading in Inner City Johannesburg" Report for Centre for Applied Legal Studies, University of the Witwatersrand, 2009; J. Cohen, "How the Global Economic Crisis Reaches Marginalised Workers: The Case of Street Traders in Johannesburg, South Africa" *Gender and Development* 18(2010): 277-89; A. Horn, "Who's Out There? A Profile of Informal Traders in Four South African Central Business Districts" *Town and Regional Planning* 59(2011): 1-6; A. van Eeden, "The Geography of Informal Arts and Crafts Traders in South Africa's Four Main City Centres" *Town and Regional Planning* 59(2011): 34-40; C. Callaghan, "Individual Values and Economic Performance of Inner-City Street Traders" *Journal of Economics* 4(2013): 145-56; A. van Eeden, "The Geography of Informal Arts and Crafts Traders in South Africa's Four Main City Centres" *Town and Regional Planning* 59(2011): 34-40; C. Hungwe, "Zimbabwean Migrant Entrepreneurs in Kempton Park and Tembisa, Johannesburg: Challenges and Opportunities" *Journal of Enterprising Culture* 22(2014): 349-73.

36  A. Ligthelm and S. van Zyl, "Profile Study of Spaza Retailers in Tembisa" Research Report No. 249, Bureau of Market Research/University of South

Africa, Johannesburg. 1998; A. Ligthelm, "Informal Retailing Through Home-Based Micro-Enterprises: The Role of Spaza Shops" *Development Southern Africa* 22(2005): 199-214; T. Chebelyon, L. Dalizu, Z.Garbowitz, A. Hause and D. Thomas, "Strengthening Spaza Shops in Monwabisi Park, Cape Town" Worcester Polytechnic Institute. Worcester MA, 2010; J. Beneke, M. Curran, G. Forsyth and S. Lamb, "Towards an Understanding of Retailing Practices in the Second Economy: An Exploratory Study of Western and Eastern Cape Township Retailers in South Africa" *African Journal of Business and Economic Research* 6(2011): 92-108; A. Charman, L. Petersen and L. Piper, "Spaza Shops in Delft: The Changing Face of Township Entrepreneurship" Sustainable Livelihoods Foundation (SLF), Cape Town, 2011; C. Abdi, "Moving Beyond Xenophobia: Structural Violence, Conflict and Encounters with the 'Other' Africans" *Development Southern Africa* 28(2011): 691-704; SLF, "The Informal Economy of Township Spaza Shops" at http://livelihoods.org.za/wp-content/uploads/2011/08/SLF-Spaza-final.pdf

37 J. Barrett, "A Case Study of the Minibus Taxi Industry in South Africa" SEED Working Paper No. 39, International Labour Office, Geneva, 2003; C. Venter, "The Lurch Towards Formalisation: Lessons from the Implementation of BRT in Johannesburg, South Africa" *Research in Transportation Economics* 39(2013): 114-20.

38 F. Miraftab, "Neoliberalism and Casualization of Public Sector Services: The Case of Waste Collection Services in Cape Town, South Africa" *International Journal of Urban and Regional Research* 28 (2004): 874-92; B. Langenhoven and M. Dyssel, "The Recycling Industry and Subsistence Waste Collectors: A Case Study of Mitchell's Plain" *Urban Forum* 18 (2007): 114-32; K. Benson and N. Vanqa-Mgijima, "Organizing on the Streets: A Study of Reclaimers in the Streets of Cape Town" Organizing Brief, No. 4, WIEGO and ILRIG, Cape Town, 2010; K. Sentime, "Informal Waste Collection in Greater Johannesburg: A Sustainable Solution?" M.A. Thesis, University of Johannesburg, 2011; M. Samson, "Wasting Value and Valuing Waste: Insights into the Global Crisis and the Production of Value Reclaimed from a Soweto Garbage Dump" PhD Thesis, York University, 2012; see also R. Schenck and P. Blauw, "The Work and Lives of Street Waste Pickers in Pretoria: Case Study of Recycling in South Africa's Urban Informal Economy" *Urban Forum* 22(2011): 411-30.

39 S. Kalichman, M. Watt, K. Sikkema, D. Skinner and D. Pieterse, "Food Insufficiency, Substance Use, and Sexual Risks for HIV/AIDS in Informal Drinking Establishments, Cape Town, South Africa" *Journal of Urban Health* 89(2012): 939-51; C. Herrick and A. Charman, "Shebeens and Crime: The Multiple Criminalities of South African Liquor and Its Regulation" *South African Crime Quarterly* 45(2013); C. Herrick and S. Parnell, "Alcohol, Poverty and the South African City" *SAGJ* 96(2014): 1-14; A. Charman, L. Petersen and T. Govender, "Shebeens as Spaces and Places of Informality, Enterprise, Drinking and Sociability" *SAGJ* 96(2014): 31-49; SLF, "Informal Liquor Retailing" at http://livelihoods.org.za/wp-content/uploads/2011/08/SLF-Informal-Liquor-final.pdf

40  V. Williams, E. Witkowski and K. Balkwill, "Volume and Financial Value of Species Traded in the Medicinal Plant Markets of Gauteng, South Africa" *International Journal of Sustainable Development and World Ecology* 14(2007): 584-603; L. Petersen, E. Moll, R. Collins, and M. Hockings, "Development of a Compendium of Local, Wild-Harvested Species Used in the Informal Economy Trade, Cape Town, South Africa" *Ecology and Society* 17 (2012):26; L. Petersen, A. Charman, E. Moll, R. Collins and M. Hockings, "'Bush Doctors and Wild Medicine': The Scale of Trade in Cape Town's Informal Economy of Wild-Harvested Medicine and Traditional Healing" *Society & Natural Resources* 27(2014): 315-36; L. Philander, N. Makunga and K. Esler, "The Informal Trade of Medicinal Plants by Rastafari Bush Doctors in the Western Cape of South Africa" *Economic Botany* 68(2014): 303-15; L. Petersen, E. Moll, M. Hockings and R. Collins, "Implementing Value Chain Analysis to Investigate Drivers and Sustainability of Cape Town's Informal Economy of Wild-Harvested Traditional Medicine" *Local Environment: The International Journal of Justice and Sustainability* DOI: 10.1080/13549839.2014.887667

41  I. Nemasetoni and C. Rogerson, "Developing Small Firms in Township Tourism: Emerging Tour Operators in Gauteng, South Africa" *Urban Forum* 16(2005):196-213; C. Rogerson, "Shared Growth in Urban Tourism: Evidence from Soweto, South Africa" *Urban Forum* 19(2008): 395–411; K. Koens, "Competition, Co-operation and Collaboration in Township Tourism: Experiences Studies from South Africa" In F. Frenzel, K. Koens and M. Steinbrink, eds., *Slum Tourism: Poverty, Power and Ethics* (London: Routledge, 2012), pp. 83-100.

42  G. Lizarralde and D. Root, "The Informal Construction Sector and the Inefficiency of Low Cost Housing Markets" *Construction Management and Economics* 26(2008): 103-13; J. Wells and A. Jason, "Employment Relationships and Organizing Strategies in the Informal Construction Sector" *African Studies Quarterly* 11(2010): 107-24.

43  Van Eeden, "Geography of Informal Arts and Crafts Traders"; SLF, "Understanding South Africa's Informal Economy" at http://livelihoods.org.za/wp-content/uploads/2011/08/SLF-Informal-Economy-Overview-final.pdf; J. Battersby and S. Peyton, "The Geography of Supermarkets in Cape Town: Supermarket Expansion and Food Access" *Urban Forum* 25(2) (2014): 153-64.

44  R. Devey, C. Skinner and I. Valodia, "Second Best? Trends and Linkages in the Informal Economy in South Africa" Working Paper 06/102, Development Policy Research Unit, University of Cape Town, 2007; R. Davies and J. Thurlow, "Formal-Informal Economy Linkages and Unemployment in South Africa" Discussion Paper 943, International Food Policy Research Institute, Washington DC, 2009.

45  J. Crush and B. Frayne, "Supermarket Expansion and the Informal Food Economy in Southern African Cities: Implications for Urban Food Security" *Journal of Southern African Studies* 37(2011): 781-807.

46  A. Louw, D. Chikazunga, D. Jordaan and E. Biénabe, "Restructuring Food Markets in South Africa: Dynamics within the Context of the Tomato Subsector" Agrifood Sector Studies, Regoverning Markets Project, University of Pretoria, 2007, p. 25; see also D. Tustin and J. Strydom, "The Potential Impact of Formal Retail Chains' Expansion on Retail Township Development in South Africa" *South African Business Review Journal* 10(2006): 48-66.

47  H. Madevu, "Competition in the Tridimensional Urban Fresh Produce Retail Market: The Case of the Tshwane Metropolitan Area, South Africa" M.Sc. Thesis, University of Pretoria, 2007.

48  A. Mathenjwa, "The Impact of Jabulani Shopping Mall on Small Township Business and Their Response" MBA Thesis, University of Pretoria, 2007; G. Zondi, "Investigating the Social and Economic Effect of Jabulani and Maponya Malls on the Residents of Soweto" MBA Thesis, Stellenbosch University, 2011.

49  C. Ngiba, D. Dickinson, L. Whittaker and C. Beswick, "Dynamics of Trade Between the Formal Sector and Informal Traders: The Case of Fruit and Vegetable Sellers at Natalspruit Market, Ekurhuleni" *South African Journal of Economic and Management Sciences* 12(2009); D. Dickinson, L. Whittaker, G. Bick, D. Benjamin, A. Bruyns, N. Kolbe, R. Mayet, N. Ngiba, D. Schraader and M. Van Steenderen, "The Informal Economy and Its Development: The Case of the Natalspruit Trading Area, Ekuhuleni" Working Paper Series No. 4, Centre for Entrepreneurship, Wits Business School, Johannesburg, 2009.

50  J. Battersby, *The State of Urban Food Insecurity in Cape Town*, AFSUN Report No. 11, Cape Town, 2011; M. Rudolph, F. Kroll, S. Ruysenaar and T. Dlamini, *The State of Urban Food Insecurity in Johannesburg*, AFSUN Report No. 12, Cape Town, 2012.

51  D. Woodward, R. Rolfe and A. Ligthelm, "Microenterprise, Multinational Business Support, and Poverty Alleviation in South Africa's Informal Economy" *Journal of African Business* 15(2014): 25-35.

52  R. Brand, "Development of a Business Framework to Integrate Informal SMMEs and Entrepreneurs with the Formal South African Economy" MSc, Stellenbosch University, 2006; W. Bradford, "Distinguishing Economically from Legally Formal Firms: Targeting Business Support to Entrepreneurs in South Africa's Townships" *Journal of Small Business Management* 45 (2007): 94-115; E. van Rooyen and A. Antonites, "Formalising the Informal Sector: A Case Study on the City of Johannesburg" *Journal of Public Administration* 42(2007): 324-46; C. Rogerson, "Tracking SMME Development in South Africa: Issues of Finance, Training and the Regulatory Environment" *Urban Forum* 19(2008): 61-81.

53  M. Chen, "The Informal Economy: Definitions, Theories and Policies" WIEGO Working Paper No. 1, 2012, p. 15.

54  A. Charman, L. Petersen and L. Piper, "Enforced Informalisation: The Case of Liquor Retailers in South Africa" *Development Southern Africa* 30(2013): 580-95.

55  H. Tamukamoyo, "Survival in a Collapsing Economy: A Case Study of Informal

Trading at a Zimbabwean Flea Market" PhD Thesis, University of the Witwatersrand, Johannesburg, 2009; T. Gumbo, "On Ideology Change and Spatial and Structural Linkages Between Formal and Informal Economic Sectors in Zimbabwean Cities (1981-2010)" PhD Thesis, Stellenbosch University, Stellenbosch, 2013.

56 G. Dube, "A Study of the Self-Employed in the Urban Informal Sector in Harare" MA Thesis, University of KwaZulu-Natal, Durban, 2010, p. 17.

57 A. Kamete, "Home Industries and the Formal City in Harare, Zimbabwe" In Hansen and Vaa, *Reconsidering Informality*; ILO, "Employment, Unemployment and Informality in Zimbabwe: Concepts and Data for Coherent Policy-Making" Integration Working Paper No. 90, ILO, Harare, 2008.

58 ZimStat, "2011 Labour Force Survey" Harare, 2012 at http://www.zimstat.co.zw/dmdocuments/Laborforce.pdf

59 Dube, "Study of the Self-Employed", p. 15.

60 J. Jones, "'Nothing is Straight in Zimbabwe': The Rise of the *Kukiya-kiya* Economy 2000–2008" *Journal of Southern African Studies* 36(2010): 285-99; A. Weston, "Creativity in the Informal Economy of Zimbabwe" PhD Thesis, Kingston, London, 2012; E. Ndiweni and H. Verhoeven, "The Rise of Informal Entrepreneurs in Zimbabwe: Evidence of Economic Growth or Failure of Economic Policies?" *African Journal of Accounting, Auditing and Finance* 2(2013): 260-76.

61 M. Luebker, "Decent Work and Informal Employment: A Survey of Workers in Glen View, Harare" Integration Working Paper No. 91, ILO, Harare, 2008.

62 Dube, "Study of the Self-Employed."

63 F. de Vletter, "Study on the Informal Sector in Mozambique" Report for Ministry of Finance and Planning, Maputo, 1996.

64 B. Byiers, "Informality in Mozambique: Characteristics, Performance and Policy Issues" Report for USAID, Washington, 2009, p. 6.

65 M. Paulo, C. Rosário and I. Tvedten, " "Xiculungo": Social Relations of Urban Poverty in Maputo, Mozambique" Report for Chr. Michelsen Institute, Bergen, 2007.

66 L. Dana and C. Gailbraith, "Poverty, Developing Entrepreneurship and Aid Economics in Mozambique: A Review of Empirical Research" *International Research in the Business Disciplines* 5 (2006): 187-201; A. Cappiello, "Estimating the Non Observed Economy in Mozambique" *Journal of Economic and Social Measurement* 33 (2008): 63-87.

67 N. Matsinhe, D. Juízo, B. Macheve and C. dos Santos "Regulation of Formal and Informal Water Service Providers in Peri-Urban Areas of Maputo" *Physics and Chemistry of the Earth, Parts A/B/C* 33 (8-13) (2008): 841-49; A. Brooks, "Riches from Rags or Persistent Poverty? The Working Lives of Secondhand Clothing Vendors in Maputo, Mozambique" *Textile* 10 (2010): 222-37; R. Brouwer, "Mobile Phones in Mozambique: The Street Trade in Airtime in Maputo City" *Science Technology Society* 15(2010): 135-54; R. Albers, V. Guida, M. Rusca and K. Schwartz, "Unleashing Entrepreneurs or Controlling Unruly Pro-

viders? The Formalisation of Small-Scale Water Providers in Greater Maputo, Mozambique" *Journal of Development Studies* 49(2013): 470-82; J. Bhatt, "Comparison of Small-Scale Providers' and Utility Performance in Urban Water Supply: The Case of Maputo, Mozambique" *Water Policy* 16(2014): 102-23; V. Zuin, L. Ortolano and J. Davis, "The Entrepreneurship Myth in Small-Scale Service Provision: Water Resale in Maputo, Mozambique" *Journal of Water, Sanitation and Hygiene for Development* 4(2014): 281-92.

68    J. Crush "Southern Hub: The Globalization of Migration to South Africa" In R. Lucas, ed., *International Handbook on Migration and Economic Development* (New York: Edward Elgar, 2015).

69    Statistics South Africa, "Tourism 2013" (Pretoria: Statistics South Africa, 2014).

70    D. Budlender, "Improving the Quality of Available Statistics on Foreign Labour in South Africa: Existing Data-Sets" MiWORC Report No. 2, ACMS, University of the Witwatersrand, Johannesburg, 2013, p. 58.

71    Personal Communication, G. Tawodzera.

72    Statistics South Africa, "Tourism, 2013" Pretoria, 2014, p. 23.

73    Ibid.

74    Cited in Budlender, "Improving the Quality of Available Statistics on Foreign Labour in South Africa."

75    Ibid., p. 52.

76    J. Crush and D. Tevera, eds., *Zimbabwe's Exodus: Crisis, Migration, Survival* (Ottawa and Cape Town: IDRC and SAMP, 2010).

77    Budlender, "Improving the Quality of Available Statistics."

78    R. Amit, "The Zimbabwean Documentation Process: Lessons Learned" African Centre for Migration and Society, Wits University, 2011.

79    J. Crush, A. Chikanda and G. Tawodzera, *The Third Wave: Mixed Migration from Zimbabwe to South Africa*, SAMP Migration Policy Series No. 59, Cape Town, 2012.

80    J. Crush, A. Jeeves and D. Yudelman, *South Africa's Labor Empire: A History of Black Migrancy to the Gold Mines* (Cape Town: David Philip, 1992); F. de Vletter, "Labour Migration to South Africa: The Lifeblood of Southern Mozambique" In D. McDonald, ed., *On Borders: Perspectives on International Migration in Southern Africa* (Cape Town: SAMP, 2000), pp. 46-70.

81    C. Mather, "Foreign Migrants in Export Agriculture: Mozambican Labour in the Mpumalanga Lowveld, South Africa" *Tijdschrift voor Economische en Sociale Geografie* 91(2000): 426-36; T. Polzer Ngwato, "Negotiating Belonging: The Integration of Mozambican Refugees in South Africa" PhD Thesis, London School of Economics and Political Science, London, 2012.

82    N. Johnston, "The Point of No Return: Evaluating the Amnesty for Mozambican Refugees in South Africa" SAMP Migration Policy Brief No. 6, Cape Town, 2001.

83  R. Muanamoha, "The Dynamics of Undocumented Mozambican Labour Migration to South Africa" PhD Thesis, University of KwaZulu-Natal, Durban, 2008; R. Muanamoha, B. Maharaj and E. Preston-Whyte, "Social Networks and Undocumented Mozambican Migration to South Africa" *Geoforum* 41 (2010): 885-96; D. Vidal, "Living in, out of, and Between Two Cities: Migrants from Maputo in Johannesburg" *Urban Forum* 21(2010): 55–68.

84  Peberdy and Rogerson, "South Africa: Creating New Spaces?"; A. Visser, "Race, Poverty, and State Intervention in the Informal Economy: Evidence from South Africa" PhD Thesis, New School University, New York, 2010; A. Wafer, "Informality, Infrastructure and the State in Post-apartheid Johannesburg" PhD Thesis, Open University, 2011.

85  P. Ragunanan and R. Smit, "Seeking Refuge in South Africa: Challenges Facing a Group of Congolese and Burundian Refugees" *Development Southern Africa* 28(2011): 705-18; D. Thompson, "Bridging the Divided City: Immigrant Economies and the Ethics of Spatial Organization in Johannesburg" MA Thesis, University of Miami, 2012; N. Radipere, "An Analysis of Local and Immigrant Entrepreneurship in the South African Small Enterprise Sector (Gauteng Province)" PhD Thesis, University of South Africa, 2012; R. Beremauro, "Living Between Compassion and Domination?: An Ethnographic Study of Institutions, Interventions and the Everyday Practices of Poor Black Zimbabwean Migrants in South Africa" PhD Thesis, University of the Witwatersrand, Johannesburg, 2013; C. Lapah and R. Tengeh, "The Migratory Trajectories of the Post-1994 Generation of African Immigrants to South Africa: An Empirical Study of Street Vendors in the Cape Town Metropolitan Area" *Mediterranean Journal of Social Sciences* 4(2013): 181-95; R. Tengeh and C. Lapah, "The Socio-Economic Trajectories of Migrant Street Vendors in Urban South Africa" *Mediterranean Journal of Social Sciences* 4(2013): 109-127.

86  R. Tengeh, H. Ballard and A. Slabbert, "Financing the Start-Up and Operation of Immigrant-Owned Businesses: The Path Taken by African Immigrants in the Cape Town Metropolitan Area of South Africa" MPRA Paper No. 38405, Munich, 2011; C. Callaghan, "The Effect of Financial Capital on Inner-City Street Trading" *Journal of Economic and Financial Sciences* 5(2011): 83-102; C. Hungwe, "Survival Strategies of Zimbabwean Migrants in Johannesburg" *Journal of Community Positive Practices* 13(2013): 52-73; L. Willemse, "Trading Hope: Working Conditions of Sub-Saharan Immigrant Street Traders in Johannesburg and Tshwane" *Africa Insight* 42(2013): 166-85; I. Moyo, "A Case Study of Black African Immigrant Entrepreneurship in Inner City Johannesburg Using the Mixed Embededness Approach" *Journal of Immigrant and Refugee Studies* 12(2014): 250-73; C. Callaghan, "Changes in the Structure of Earnings of Informal Street Traders" *Acta Commercii* 14(2014).

87  O. Fatoki, "An Investigation into the Financial Bootstrapping Methods Used by Immigrant Entrepreneurs in South Africa" *Journal of Economics* 4(2013): 89-96; A. Ikuomola and J. Zaaiman, "We Have Come to Stay and We Shall Find All

Means to Live and Work in this Country: Nigerian Migrants and Life Challenges in South Africa" *Issues in Ethnology and Anthropology* 9(2014): 371-88; V. Gastrow and R. Amit, "Somalinomics: A Case Study on the Economic Dimensions of Somali Informal Trade in the Western Cape" ACMS Report, University of the Witwatersrand, 2013.

88 A. Morris, "'Our Fellow Africans Make Our Lives Hell': The Lives of Congolese and Nigerians Living in Johannesburg" *Ethnic and Racial Studies* 21(1998): 1116-1136; Peberdy and Rogerson, "Transnationalism and Non-South African Entrepreneurs"; Peberdy and Rogerson, "South Africa: Creating New Spaces?"

89 N. Hunter and C. Skinner, "Foreigners Working on the Streets of Durban: Local Government Policy Challenges" *Urban Forum* 14(2003): 301-19; H. Pauw and T. Petrus, "Xenophobia and Informal Trading in Port Elizabeth" *Anthropology Southern Africa*, 26(2003): 172-180; N. Masonganye, "Street Trading in Tshwane Metropolitan Municipality: Realities and Challenge" *Urban Landmark*, Pretoria, 2009; Y. Park and A. Chen, "Recent Chinese Migrants in Small Towns of Post-Apartheid South Africa" *Revue Européenne des Migrations Internationales* 25(2009): 25-44; A. Hikam, "An Exploratory Study on the Somali Immigrants Involvement in the Informal Economy of Nelson Mandela Bay" M.Dev.Stud., Nelson Mandela University, Port Elizabeth, 2011; I. Gebre, P. Maharaj and N. Pillay, "The Experiences of Immigrants in South Africa: A Case Study of Ethiopians in Durban, South Africa" *Urban Forum* 22(2011): 23-35; O. Fatoki and T. Patswawairi, "The Motivations and Obstacles to Immigrant Entrepreneurship" *Journal of Social Science* 32(2012): 133-42; N. Sidzatane and P. Maharaj, "On the Fringe of the Economy: Migrant Street Traders in Durban" *Urban Forum* 24(2013): 373-87; D. Mthombeni, F. Anim and B. Nkonki-Mandleni, "Factors That Contribute to Vegetable Sales by Hawkers in the Limpopo Province of South Africa" *Journal of Agricultural Science* 6(2014): 197-204; A. Garg and N. Phayane, "Impact of Small Businesses Owned By Immigrant Entrepreneurs on the Local Community of Brits" *Journal of Small Business and Entrepreneurship Development* 2(2014): 57-85.

90 Skinner, "Street Trade in Africa."

91 Crush et al., *The Third Wave*.

92 Z. Jinnah, "Making Home in a Hostile Land: Understanding Somali Identity, Integration, Livelihood and Risks in Johannesburg" *Journal of Sociology and Social Anthropology* 1 (2010): 91-9; Gastrow and Amit, "Somalinomics".

93 V. Maqanda, "Competitiveness of Small Businesses Owned by Asians and Expatriate Africans in South Africa Compared to those Owned by Indigenous Citizens" M.Com. Thesis, University of South Africa, 2012.

94 Van Rooyen and Antonites, "Formalising the Informal Sector" p. 337.

95 D. Budlender, "Migration and Employment in South Africa: Statistical Analysis of the Migration Module in the Quarterly Labour Force Survey, Third Quarter 2012" MiWORC Report, Johannesburg, 2014.

96 T. Huynh, Y. Park and A. Chen, "Faces of China: New Chinese Migrants in

South Africa, 1980s to Present" *African and Asian Studies* 9(2010): 286-306; S. Govender, "The Socio-Economic Participation of Chinese Migrant Traders in the City of Durban" M.Soc.Sci., University of KwaZulu-Natal, Durban, 2012; P. Harrison, K. Moyo and Y. Yang, "Strategy and Tactics: Chinese Immigrants and Diasporic Spaces in Johannesburg, South Africa" *Journal of Southern African Studies* 38(2012): 899-924; T. McNamee, "Africa in Their Words: A Study of Chinese Traders in South Africa, Lesotho, Botswana, Zambia and Angola" Discussion Paper 2013/3, Brenthurst Foundation, Johannesburg, 2012; N. Munshi, "Lived Experiences and Local Spaces: Bangladeshi Migrants in Post-Apartheid South Africa" *New Contree* 67(2013): 119-37; E. Lin, "'Big Fish in a Small Pond': Chinese Migrant Shopkeepers in South Africa" *International Migration Review* 48(2014): 181-215; L. Willemse, "The Role of Economic Factors and Guanxi Networks in the Success of Chinese Shops in Johannesburg, South Africa" *Urban Forum* 25(2014): 105-23.

97   C. Rogerson, "International Migration, Immigrant Entrepreneurs and South Africa's Small Enterprise Economy" SAMP Migration Policy Series No. 3, Cape Town, 1997; S. Peberdy and C. Rogerson, "Transnationalism and Non-South African Entrepreneurs in South Africa's Small, Medium and Micro-Enterprise (SMME) Economy" In J. Crush and D. McDonald, eds., *Transnationalism and New African Immigration to South Africa* (Toronto, 2002), pp. 20-40; S. Peberdy and C. Rogerson, "South Africa: Creating New Spaces?" In R. Kloosterman and J. Rath, eds., *Immigrant Entrepreneurs: Venturing Abroad in the Age of Globalization* (Oxford, 2003), pp. 79-100.

98   N. Hunter and C. Skinner, "Foreign Street Traders Working in Inner City Durban: Local Government Policy Challenges" *Urban Forum* 14 (2003): 301-19; C. Skinner, "Falling though the Policy Gaps? Evidence from the Informal Economy in Durban, South Africa" *Urban Forum* 17 (2006): 125-48; B. Maharaj, "Migrants and Urban Rights: Politics of Xenophobia in South African Cities" *L'Espace Politique* 8 (2009); J. Crush and S. Ramachandran, "Xenophobia, International Migration and Development" *Journal of Human Development and Capabilities* 11(2) (2010): 209-28.

99   J. Crush and S. Ramachandran, *Xenophobic Violence in South Africa: Denialism, Minimalism, Realism*, SAMP Migration Policy Series No. 66, Cape Town, 2014; J. Crush and S. Ramachandran, *Migrant Entrepreneurship and Collective Violence in South Africa*, SAMP Migration Policy Series No. 67, Cape Town, 2014.

100  Fatoki, "Financial Bootstrapping Methods" pp. 92-3; also O. Fatoki, "The Impact of Entrepreneurial Orientation on Access to Debt Finance and Performance of Small and Medium Enterprises in South Africa" *Journal of Social Science* 32(2012): 121-31.

101  Ibid.

102  R. Tengeh, "A Business Framework for the Effective Start-Up and Operation of African Immigrant-Owned Businesses in the Cape Town Metropolitan Area, South Africa" PhD Thesis, Cape Peninsula University of Technology, 2012, p. 206.

103 R. Khosa, "An Analysis of Challenges in Running Micro-Enterprises: A Case of African Foreign Entrepreneurs in Cape Town, Western Cape" M.Tech. Thesis, Cape Peninsula University of Technology, Cape Town, 2014.

104 Fatoki "Financial Bootstrapping Methods."

105 R. Tengeh, H. Ballard and A. Slabbert, "Do Immigrant-owned Businesses Grow Financially?: An Empirical Study of African Immigrant-Owned Businesses in South Africa" MPRA Paper No. 40610, Munich, 2012.

106 O. Fatoki, "The Competitive Intelligence Activity of Immigrant Entrepreneurs in South Africa" *Journal of Social Sciences* 38(2014): 1-8.

107 C. Callaghan, "Values Malleability or the Potentially Harmful Effects of Exposure to Street Trading? Derived GLOBE Individual Values, Context and Informal Entrepreneurial Outcomes in the African Street Trading Context" *Journal of Business Management* 6(2012): 8362-77.

108 C. Callaghan and R. Venter, "An Investigation of the Entrepreneurial Orientation, Context and Entrepreneurial Performance of Inner-City Johannesburg Street Traders" *Southern African Business Review* 15(2011): 28-48; Fatoki, "The Determinants of Immigrant Entrepreneurs Growth Expectations in South Africa."

109 N. Hyde-Clarke, "The Impact of Mobile Technology on Economic Growth Among 'Survivalists' in the Informal Sector in the Johannesburg CBD, South Africa" *International Journal of Business and Social Science* 4(2013): 149-156.

110 O. Fatoki, "Working Capital Management Practices of Immigrant Entrepreneurs in South Africa" *Mediterranean Journal of Social Sciences* 5(2014): 52-57.

111 V. Kalitanyi and K. Visser, "African Immigrants in South Africa: Job Takers or Job Creators?" *South African Journal of Economic and Management Sciences* 13(2010): 376-90.

112 M. Morris and L. Pitt, "Informal Sector Activity as Entrepreneurship: Insights from a South African Township" *Journal of Small Business Management* 33(1995): 78-86; C. Callaghan, "Individual Values and Economic Performance of Inner-City Street Traders" *Journal of Economics* 4(2013): 145-56.

113 A. Doyle, A. Peters and A. Sundaram, "Skills Mismatch and Informal Sector Participation Among Skilled Immigrants: Evidence from South Africa" SALD-RU Working Paper No. 137, University of Cape Town, 2014, p. 4.

114 C. Rogerson, *International Migration, Immigrant Entrepreneurs and South Africa's Small Enterprise Economy*, SAMP Migration Policy Series No. 3, Cape Town, 1997.

115 Kalitanyi and Visser, "African Immigrants in South Africa."

116 Tengeh, "Business Framework for African Immigrant-Owned Businesses."

117 Ibid., p. 220.

118 V. Kalitanyi, "Evaluation of Employment Creation by African Immigrant Entrepreneurs for Unemployed South Africans in Cape Town" M.Comm. Thesis, University of Western Cape, 2007, p. 76.

119 N. Radipere, "An Analysis of Local and Immigrant Entrepreneurship in the

South African Small Enterprise Sector (Gauteng Province)" PhD Thesis, University of South Africa, 2012.

120 Ibid., p. 183.

121 C. Rogerson, "Urban Tourism and Regional Tourists: Shopping in Johannesburg, South Africa" *Tijdschrift voor Economische en Sociale Geografie* 102 (2010): 316-30; C. Rogerson, "Informal Sector Business Tourism and Pro-Poor Tourism: Africa's Migrant Entrepreneurs" *Mediterranean Journal of Social Sciences* 5(2014): 153-61.

122 M. Desai, "Women Cross-Border Traders: Rethinking Global Trade" *Development* 52(2009): 377–86; C. Lesser and E. Moisé-Leeman, "Informal Cross-Border Trade and Trade Facilitation Reform in Sub-Saharan Africa" OECD Trade Policy Working Papers No. 86, Paris, 2009.

123 O. Akinboade, "A Review of Women, Poverty, and Informal Trade Issues in East and Southern Africa" *International Social Science Journal* 57(2005): 255–75.

124 S. Peberdy and J. Crush, *Trading Places: Cross Border Traders and the South African Informal Sector*, SAMP Migration Policy Series No. 6, Cape Town, 1998; D. Dlela, "Informal Cross Border Trade: The Case for Zimbabwe" Occasional Paper No. 52, Institute for Global Dialogue, Johannesburg, 2006; S. Peberdy et al., "Monitoring Small Scale Cross Border Trade in Southern Africa" SAMP Report for Regional Trade Facilitation Programme, Cape Town, 2007.

125 S. Peberdy and J. Crush, *Trading Places: Cross Border Traders and the South African Informal Sector*, SAMP Migration Policy Series No. 6, Cape Town, 1998; S. Peberdy and J. Crush, "Invisible Trade, Invisible Travellers: The Maputo Corridor Spatial Development Initiative and Informal Cross-Border Trading," *South African Geographical Journal*, 83(2001): 115-123; V. Muzvidziwa, "Women Without Borders: Informal Cross Border Trade among Women in the Southern African Development Community Region (SADC)" Organisation for Social Science Research in Eastern and Southern Africa (OSSREA), Addis Ababa, Ethiopia, 2005; J. Mijere, "Informal Cross-Border Trade in the Southern African Development Community (SADC)" OSSREA, Addis Ababa, Ethiopia, 2006; S. Peberdy at al., "Monitoring Small Scale Cross Border Trade in Southern Africa" SAMP Report for Regional Trade Facilitation Programme, Cape Town, 2007; Skinner, "Street Trade in Africa."

126 J-G. Afrika and G. Ajumbo, "Informal Cross Border Trade in Africa: Implications and Policy Recommendations" *Africa Economic Brief* 3(2012), p. 4.

127 FEWSNET, "Informal Cross Border Food Trade in Southern Africa", Famine Early Warning Systems Network, Pretoria, 2012.

128 Ibid.

129 Peberdy et al., "Monitoring Small Scale Cross Border Trade in Southern Africa."

130 Ibid.

131 Ibid.

132 SBP, "Cross-Border African Shoppers and Traders in South Africa: Findings from an SBP Survey" SME Alert, January 2006 at http://www.sbp.org.za/uploads/media/SME_Alert_Cross_Border_Shopping_final_8-12-06.pdf

133 Ibid., p. 4.

134 Ibid.

135 Ibid., p. 5.

136 V. Muzvidziwa, "Zimbabwe's Cross-Border Women Traders: Multiple Identities and Responses to New Challenges" *Journal of Comparative African Studies*, 19(2001): 67-80; R. Mupedziswa and P. Gumbo, "Women Informal Traders in Harare and the Struggle for Survival in an Environment of Economic Reforms" Research Report No. 117, Nordiska Afrikainstitutet, Uppsala, 2001; D. Dlela, "Informal Cross Border Trade: The Case for Zimbabwe" Occasional Paper No. 52, Institute for Global Dialogue, Johannesburg, 2006; P. Mazengwa, "A Business Analysis of Zimbabwean Cross Border Trading" MA Thesis, University of KwaZulu-Natal, Durban, 2003; C. Chivani, "Informal Cross-Border Trade: A Review of Its Impact on Household Poverty Reduction (Zimbabwe)" M.Soc. Sci. Thesis, University of Fort Hare, 2008; W. Kachere, "Informal Cross Border Trading and Poverty Reduction in the Southern African Development Community: The Case of Zimbabwe" PhD Thesis, University of Fort Hare, 2011; N. Ciliva, R. Masocha and S. Zindiye, "Challenges Facing Zimbabwean Cross Border Traders Trading in South Africa: A Review of the Literature" *Chinese Business Review* 12(2011): 564-70; T. Jamela, "Experiences and Coping Strategies of Women Informal Cross-Border Traders in Unstable Political and Economic Conditions: The Case of Bulawayo (Zimbabwe) Traders" M.Dev.Stud., University of Johannesburg, 2013.

137 S. Peberdy, "Border Crossings: Small Enterpreneurs and Cross-Border Trade between South Africa and Mozambique" *Tijdschrift voor Economische en Sociale Geografie* 91(2001): 361-78; Peberdy and Crush, "Invisible Trade, Invisible Travellers"; F. Söderbaum, "Blocking Human Potential: How Formal Policies Block the Informal Economy in the Maputo Corridor" In B. Guha-Khasnobis, R. Kanbur and E. Ostrom, eds., *Linking the Formal and Informal Economy* (Oxford: OUP, 2006); D. Vidal, "Living in, Out of, and Between Two Cities: Migrants from Maputo in Johannesburg" *Urban Forum* 21(2010): 55-68.

138 K. Lefko-Everett, *Voices from the Margins: Migrant Women's Experiences in Southern Africa*, SAMP Migration Policy Series No. 46, Cape Town, 2007.

139 DPC & Associates, "Report on Regional Cross Border Trade Stakeholder Dialogue" Maputo, 2013, pp. 25-6.

140 Lefko-Everett, *Voices from the Margins*.

141 J. Crush and W. Pendleton, "Remitting for Survival: Rethinking the Development Potential of Remittances in Southern Africa" *Global Development Studies* 5(2009): 53-84; B. Frayne and W. Pendleton, "The Development Role of Remittances in the Urbanization Process in Southern Africa" *Global Development Studies* 5(2009): 85-132; D. Tevera, J. Crush and A. Chikanda, "Migrant Remittances and Household Survival in Zimbabwe" In Crush and Tevera, *Zimbabwe's Exodus*, pp. 307-321; S. Bracking and L. Sachikonye, "Remittances, Informalisation and Dispossession in Urban Zimbabwe" In Crush and Tevera, *Zimbabwe's*

*Exodus*, pp. 324-343; D. Makina, "Migration and Characteristics of Remittance Senders in South Africa" *International Migration* 51(2013): 148-58.

142 S. Truen and S. Chisadza, "The South Africa-SADC Remittance Channel" FinMark Trust, Pretoria, 2012.

143 W. Pendleton, J. Crush, E. Campbell, T. Green, H. Simelane, D. Tevera and F. de Vletter, *Migration, Remittances and Development in Southern Africa*, SAMP Migration Policy Series No. 44, Cape Town, 2006.

144 V. Thebe, "From South Africa with Love: The Malayisha System and Ndebele Households' Quest for Livelihood Reconstruction in South-Western Zimbabwe" *Journal of Modern African Studies* 49(2011): 647-670.

145 Ibid., p. 667.

146 Pendleton et al., *Migration,Remittances and Development in Southern Africa*, p. 26.

147 B. Dodson, H. Simelane, D. Tevera, T. Green, A. Chikanda and F. de Vletter, *Gender, Migration and Remittances in Southern Africa*, SAMP Migration Policy Series No. 49, Cape Town, 2008.

148 B. Dodson, *Women on the Move: Gender and Cross-Border Migration to South Africa*, SAMP Migration Policy Series No. 9, Cape Town, 1998; B. Dodson, "Women on the Move: Gender and Cross-Border Migration to South Africa from Lesotho, Mozambique and Zimbabwe" In D. McDonald, ed., *On Borders: Perspectives on International Migration in Southern Africa* (New York and Cape Town: St Martin's Press and SAMP, 2000); B. Dodson, "Gender, Migration and Livelihoods: Migrant Women in Southern Africa" In N. Piper, ed., *New Perspectives on Gender and Migration: Livelihood, Rights and Entitlements* (London: Routledge, 2007).

149 R. Mayet, "Challenges Facing Women Street Traders in the Informal Economy" MBA Research Report, Wits Business School, Johannesburg, 2007; T. Berry, "Challenges and Coping Strategies of Female Street Vendors in the Informal Economy" MA Thesis, University of Pretoria, 2009; A. Mugisho, "The Socio-Economic Integration of Congolese Migrants in Johannesburg: A Gendered Analysis" MA Thesis, University of the Witwatersrand, 2011; R. Grant, "Gendered Spaces of Informal Entrepreneurship in Soweto, South Africa" *Urban Geography* 34(2013): 86-108. C. Callaghan, "Development and Gender: Longitudinal Entrepreneurial Gender Effects of the Inner City Johannesburg Street Trading Context" *Development Southern Africa* 31(2014): 412-26.

150 R. Mupedziswa and P. Gumbo, "Women Informal Traders in Harare and the Struggle for Survival in an Environment of Economic Reforms" Research Report No. 117, Nordiska Afrikainstitutet, 2001.

151 O. Manyanhaire, T. Murenje, P. Chibisa, D. Munasirei and E. Svotwa, "Investigating Gender Dimensions in Vending Activities in the City of Mutare, Zimbabwe" *Journal of Sustainable Development in Africa* 9(2007): 169-86; T. Chirau, "Understanding Livelihood Strategies of Urban Women Traders: A Case of Magaba, Harare in Zimbabwe" MSocSci, Rhodes University, Grahamstown, 2012; I. Chirisa, "Peri-Urban Informal Trading in Zimbabwe: A Case Study of

Women in the Sector (WIIS) in Ruwa" *Journal of Global and Scientific Issues* 1(2013): 22-39; T. Chirau and P. Tamuka, "Politicisation of Urban Space: Evidence from Women Informal Traders at Magaba, Harare in Zimbabwe" *Global Advanced Research Journal of History, Political Science and International Relations* 2(2013): 14-26.

152 V. Agadjanian, "Men Doing 'Women's Work': Masculinity and Gender Relations Among Street Vendors in Maputo, Mozambique" *Journal of Men's Studies* 10(2002): 329-42; N. Monteiro, "The Political Economy of Informal Markets: Restructuring Economies, Gender and Women's Lives in Maputo, Mozambique" PhD Thesis, Northern Arizona University, Flagstaff, 2002.

153 Peberdy, "Border Crossings."

154 B. Karumbidza, "Criminalising the Livelihoods of the Poor: The Impact of Formalising Informal Trading on Female and Migrant Traders in Durban" Report for Socio-Economic Rights Institute, Durban, 2011; D. Woodward, R. Rolfe, A. Ligthelm and P. Guimarães, "The Viability of Informal Microenterprise in South Africa" *Journal of Developmental Entrepreneurship* 16(2011); O. Fatoki, "Factors Motivating Young South African Women to Become Entrepreneurs" *Mediterranean Journal of Social Sciences* 5(2014): 184-90.

155 G. Tati, "Entrepreneurial African Female Migrants at the Informal-Formal Interface of the Urban Economy: Are Gender Asymmetries Modified by Entrepreneurship?" Paper for Symposium on Gender, Migration and Socioeconomic Development in Africa, Cairo, 2010.

156 B. Dodson and J. Crush, "Report on Gender Discrimination in South Africa's 2002 Immigration Act: Masculinizing the Migrant" *Feminist Review* 77 (2004): 96-119; S. Peberdy, "The Invisible Woman: Gender Blindness and South African Immigration Policies and Legislation" *Signs* 33 (2008): 800-7.

157 F. Lund and C. Skinner, "Promoting the Interests of Women Street Traders: An Analysis of Organizations in South Africa" CSDS Research Report No. 19, Durban, 1999; C. Skinner, "Local Government in Transition – A Gendered Analysis of Trends in Urban Policy and Practice Regarding Street Trading in Five South African Cities" CSDS Research Report No. 18, Durban 1999.

158 Lefko-Everett, *Voices from the Margins.*

159 S. Shane, E. A. Locke and C. Collins, "Entrepreneurial Motivation" *Human Resource Management Review* 13(2003): 257-79; G. Segal, D. Bogia and J. Schoenfeld, "The Motivation to Become an Entrepreneur" *International Journal of Entrepreneurial Behaviour and Research* 11(2005): 42-57; A. Carsrud and M. Brännback, "Entrepreneurial Motivations: What Do We Still Need to Know?" *Journal of Small Business Management* 49(2011): 9-26.

160 Carsrud and Brännback, "Entrepreneurial Motivations."

161 B. Urban, "Researching Entrepreneurship from a Cognitive Perspective: A Focus on Necessity Entrepreneurs in the Johannesburg Area" *African Journal of Business Management* 6(2012): 11733.

162 E. Berner, G. Gomez and P. Knorringa, "'Helping a Large Number of People Become a Little Less Poor': The Logic of Survival Entrepreneurs" *European Journal of Development Research* 24(2012): 382–96; K. Adom, "Beyond the Marginalisation Thesis: An Examination of the Motivations of Informal Entrepreneurs in Sub-Saharan Africa: Insights from Ghana" *International Journal of Entrepreneurship and Innovation* 15(2014): 113-25.

163 Urban, "Researching Entrepreneurship from a Cognitive Perspective."

164 C. Callaghan, "Informal Development and Involuntary Employment" *Journal of Economics* 3(2012): 83-93.

165 C. Callaghan, "Individual Values and Economic Performance of Inner-City Street Traders" *Journal of Economics* 4(2013): 145-56.

166 O. Fatoki and L. Chindoga, "An Investigation into the Obstacles to Youth Entrepreneurship in South Africa" *International Business Research* 4 (2011): 161-9; P. Preisendörfer, A. Bitz and F. Bezuidenhout, "In Search of Black Entrepreneurship: Why Is There a Lack of Entrepreneurial Activity Among the Black Population in South Africa" *Journal of Developmental Entrepreneurship* 17(2012): 1-18.

167 J. Luiz and M. Mariotti, "Entrepreneurship in an Emerging and Culturally Diverse Economy: A South African Survey of Perceptions" *South African Journal of Economic and Management Sciences* 14(2011): 47-64; P. Preisendörfer, A. Bitz and F. Bezuidenhout, "Business Start-ups and Their Prospects of Success in South African Townships" *South African Review of Sociology* 43(2012): 3-23; P. Preisendörfer, S. Perks and F. Bezuidenhout, "Do South African Townships Lack Entrepreneurial Spirit?" *International Journal of Entrepreneurship and Small Business* 22(2014): 159-78; P. Preisendörfer, A. Bitz and F. Bezuidenhout, "Black Entrepreneurship: A Case Study on Entrepreneurial Activities and Ambitions in a South African Township" *Journal of Enterprising Communities* 8(2014): 162-79. O. Fatoki, "Factors Motivating Young South African Women to Become Entrepreneurs" *Mediterranean Journal of Social Sciences* 5(2014a): 184-190.

168 G. Kingdon and J. Knight, "Why High Open Unemployment and Small Informal Sector in South Africa?" Centre for the Study of African Economies, Oxford University 2001; N. Turton and M. Herrington, *Global Entrepreneurship Monitor 2012: South Africa* (Cape Town: UCT Business School, 2013).

169 C. Lapah and R. Tengeh, "The Migratory Trajectories of the Post-1994 Generation of African Immigrants to South Africa: An Empirical Study of Street Vendors in the Cape Town Metropolitan Area" *Mediterranean Journal of Social Sciences* 4 (2013): 181-95.

170 S. Radipere and S. Dhliwayo, "An Analysis of Local and Immigrant Entrepreneurs in South Africa's SME Sector" *Mediterranean Journal of Social Sciences* 5(2014): 189-98.

171 C. Callaghan and R. Venter, "An Investigation of the Entrepreneurial Orientation, Context and Entrepreneurial Performance of Inner-City Johannesburg

Street Traders" *Southern African Business Review* 15(2011): 28-48.

172 C. Callaghan, "Entrepreneurial Orientation and Entrepreneurial Performance of Central Johannesburg Informal Sector Street Traders" M. Comm. Thesis, University of the Witwatersrand, 2009, pp. 227, 301.

173 Ibid.

174 F. Basardien, H. Parker, M. Bayat, C. Friedrich and A. Sulaiman, "Entrepreneurial Orientation of Spaz Shop Entrepreneurs: Evidence from a Study of South African and Somali-Owned Spaza Shop Entrepreneurs in Khayelitsha" *Singaporean Journal of Business Economics and Management Studies* 2(2014): 45-61.

175 O. Fatoki, "The Competitive Intelligence Activity of Immigrant Entrepreneurs in South Africa" *Journal of Social Sciences* 38(2014): 1-8.

176 O. Fatoki, "The Determinants of Immigrant Entrepreneurs Growth Expectations in South Africa" *Journal of Social Sciences* 37(2013): 209-16.

177 A. Kamete, "Missing The Point? Urban Planning and the Normalisation of 'Pathological'Sspaces in Southern Africa" *Transactions of the Institute of British Geographers* 38(2013): 639-51.

178 D. Potts, "'Restoring Order'? Operation Murambatsvina and the Urban Crisis in Zimbabwe" *Journal of Southern African Studies* 32(2) (2006): 273-91; K. Manganga, "Street Vending in Post-Operation Murambatsvina Harare: The Case of Female Vendors at Machipisa, Highfield Township" Report for the Living on the Margins Conference, Stellenbosch, 2007; D. Potts, "Displacement and Livelihoods: The Longer Term Impacts of Operation Murambatsvina" In M. Vambe, ed., *The Hidden Dimensions of Operation Murambatsvina* (Harare: Weaver, 2008), pp. 53-64.

179 A. Tibaijuka, "Report of the Fact-Finding Mission to Zimbabwe to Assess the Scope and Impact of Operation Murambatsvina by the UN Special Envoy on Human Settlements Issues in Zimbabwe" United Nations, New York, 2005 at www.un.org/News/dh/infocus/zimbabwe/zimbabwe_rpt.pdf

180 D. Potts, "City Life in Zimbabwe at a Time of Fear and Loathing: Urban Planning, Urban Poverty and Operation Murambatsvina" In G. Myers and M. Murray, eds., *Cities in Contemporary Africa* (New York, Palgrave Macmillan, 2007), p. 265.

181 E. Ndiweni and H. Verhoeven, "The Rise of Informal Entrepreneurs in Zimbabwe: Evidence of Economic Growth or Failure of Economic Policies?" *African Journal of Accounting, Auditing and Finance* 2(2013): 260-76.

182 M. Vambe, ed., *The Hidden Dimensions of Operation Murambatsvina* (Harare: Weaver, 2008); A. Kamete and I. Lindell, "The Politics of 'Non-Planning' Interventions in African Cities: Unravelling the International and Local Dimensions in Harare and Maputo" *Journal of Southern African Studies* 36(2010): 889–912.

183 I. Chirisa, "Post-2005 Harare: A Case of the Informal Sector and Street Vending Resilience. What Options Do Key Players Have?" *Local Governance and Development Journal* 1(2007): 53-64; H. Tamukamoyo, "Survival in a Collapsing Economy: A Case Study of Informal Trading at a Zimbabwean Flea Market"

PhD Thesis, University of the Witwatersrand, Johannesburg, 2009; I. Chirisa and D. Dube, "The Informal City: Assessing its Scope, Variants and Direction in Harare, Zimbabwe" *Global Advanced Research Journal of Geography and Regional Planning* 1(2012): 16-25; T. Chirau, "Exploring Livelihoods of Urban Women Traders in the Context of Socio-economic and Political Crisis: Evidence from Harare, Zimbabwe" *Global Journal of Human Social Science* 14(2014): 77-93.

184 Kamete and Lindell, "The Politics of 'Non-Planning' Interventions in African Cities."

185 P. Dibben, G. Wood and C. Williams, "Towards and Against Formalization: Regulation and Change in Informal Work in Mozambique" *International Labour Review* DOI: 10.1111/j.1564-913X.2014.00014.x

186 Ibid.

187 Ibid.

188 F. Kaufmann and W. Parlmeyer, "The Dilemma of Small Business in Mozambique: A Research Note" *International Research in the Business Disciplines* 5 (2006): 203–14; M. Krause et al., "Business Development in Mozambique: What is the Role of the Regulatory Business Environment in Supporting Formalisation and Development of Micro, Small and Medium Enterprises?" Report of German Development Institute, Bonn, 2008; M. Krause, M. Ackermann, L. Gayoso, C. Hirtbach, M. Koppa and L. Brêtas, "Formalisation and Business Development in Mozambique" Report of German Development Institute, Bonn, 2010.

189 B. Byiers, "Enterprise Survey Evidence" In C. Arndt and F. Tarp, eds., *Taxation in a Low-Income Economy: The Case of Mozambique* ( New York: Routledge, 2009).

190 B. Byiers, "Informality in Mozambique: Characteristics, Performance and Policy Issues" Report for USAID, Washington DC, 2009.

191 A. Ulset, "Formalization of Informal Marketplaces: A Case Study of the Xikhelene Market, Maputo, Mozambique" MA Thesis, University of Oslo, 2010.

192 C. Rogerson, "The Impact of the South African Government's SMME Programme: A Ten Year Review (1994-2003)" *Development Southern Africa* 21(2004); W. Bradford, "Distinguishing Economically from Legally Formal Firms: Targeting Business Support to Entrepreneurs in South Africa's Townships" *Journal of Small Business Management* 45 (2007): 94-115.

193 R. Devey, C. Skinner and I. Valodia, "The State of the Informal Economy" In S. Buhlungu, J. Daniel, R. Southall and J. Lutchman (Eds), *The State of the Nation, 2005-2006* (Cape Town: HSRC, 2006), p. 226.

194 G. Chiloane and W. Mayhew, "Difficulties Encountered by Women Entrepreneurs in Accessing Training from the Small Enterprise Development Agency in South Africa" *Gender and Behaviour* 8 (2010): 2590-602.

195 C. Skinner, "Falling Through the Policy Gaps? Evidence from the Informal Economy in Durban, South Africa" *Urban Forum* 17(2006): 125-48.

196 Republic of South Africa, Department of Trade and Industry, "Licensing of Businesses Bill" Notice 231 of 2013.

197 Ibid, p. 10.

198 Sapa, "Foreign-Owned Businesses Hampering Rural Growth – DTI" *City Press* 10 October 2013.

199 African National Congress, "National Executive Statement" 31 March 2014.

200 City of Johannesburg, "Informal Trading Policy" 2009 at http://joburg-archive. co.za/2010/pdfs/informal_trading_policy.pdf

201 City of Cape Town, "Informal Trading Policy 2013 (Policy Number 12664)" at http://www.capetown.gov.za/en/Policies/All%20Policies/Informal%20Trading,%202013%20-%20(Policy%20number%2012664)%20approved%20on%20 26%20September%202013.pdf

202 http://www.seri-sa.org/index.php/19-litigation/case-entries/206-south-african-informal-traders-forum-and-others-v-city-of-johannesburg-and-others-saitf

203 City of Johannesburg, Council Meeting Resolution, 21 May 2014.

204 A. Wafer, "Informality, Infrastructure and the State in Post-Apartheid Johannesburg" PhD Thesis, Open University, 2011; A. Wafer, "Informality and Spaces of Civil Society in Post-Apartheid Johannesburg" In C. Gabay and C. Death, eds., *Critical Perspectives on African Politics: Liberal Interventions, State-building and Civil Society* ( London: Routledge, 2014).

205 A. Bukasa, "Securing Sustainable Livelihoods: A Critical Assessment of the City of Cape Town's Approach to Inner City Street Trading" MA Thesis, University of Cape Town, p. 53; B. Mwasinga, "Assessing the Implications of Local Governance on Street Trading: A Case of Cape Town's Inner City" Masters in City and Regional Planning Thesis, University of Cape Town, 2013.

206 See for example "Hawkers Challenge Cape Town's Swoop" *IOL News Online* 21 May 2012 and E. Weiss, "Railway Security Guards Accused of Burning Down Hawkers Goods" SA *Breaking News* 10 May 2013.

207 Abdi, "Moving Beyond Xenophobia"; Charman and Piper, "Xenophobia, Criminality and Violent Entrepreneurship"; V. Gastrow, "'Business Robbery, the Foreign Trader and the Small Shop: How Business Robberies Affect Somali Traders in the Western Cape" *South African Crime Quarterly* 43(2013): 5-15.

208 Lefko-Everett, *Voices from the Margins.*

209 A. de Haan, "Inclusive Growth? Labour Migration and Poverty in India" Working Paper No. 513, Institute of Social Studies, The Hague, 2011.

210 J. Heintz, "Informality, Inclusiveness and Economic Growth: An Overview of Key Issues" SIG Working Paper No. 2, IDRC, Ottawa, 2012; see also J. Heintz, "Employment, Poverty and Inclusive Development in Africa: Policy Choices in the Context of Widespread Informality" In V. Padayachee, ed., *The Political Economy of Africa* (London: Routledge, 2010), pp. 199-213.

## MIGRATION POLICY SERIES

1. *Covert Operations: Clandestine Migration, Temporary Work and Immigration Policy in South Africa* (1997) ISBN 1-874864-51-9

2. *Riding the Tiger: Lesotho Miners and Permanent Residence in South Africa* (1997) ISBN 1-874864-52-7

3. *International Migration, Immigrant Entrepreneurs and South Africa's Small Enterprise Economy* (1997) ISBN 1-874864-62-4

4. *Silenced by Nation Building: African Immigrants and Language Policy in the New South Africa* (1998) ISBN 1-874864-64-0

5. *Left Out in the Cold? Housing and Immigration in the New South Africa* (1998) ISBN 1-874864-68-3

6. *Trading Places: Cross-Border Traders and the South African Informal Sector* (1998) ISBN 1-874864-71-3

7. *Challenging Xenophobia: Myth and Realities about Cross-Border Migration in Southern Africa* (1998) ISBN 1-874864-70-5

8. *Sons of Mozambique: Mozambican Miners and Post-Apartheid South Africa* (1998) ISBN 1-874864-78-0

9. *Women on the Move: Gender and Cross-Border Migration to South Africa* (1998) ISBN 1-874864-82-9.

10. *Namibians on South Africa: Attitudes Towards Cross-Border Migration and Immigration Policy* (1998) ISBN 1-874864-84-5.

11. *Building Skills: Cross-Border Migrants and the South African Construction Industry* (1999) ISBN 1-874864-84-5

12. *Immigration & Education: International Students at South African Universities and Technikons* (1999) ISBN 1-874864-89-6

13. *The Lives and Times of African Immigrants in Post-Apartheid South Africa* (1999) ISBN 1-874864-91-8

14. *Still Waiting for the Barbarians: South African Attitudes to Immigrants and Immigration* (1999) ISBN 1-874864-91-8

15. *Undermining Labour: Migrancy and Sub-contracting in the South African Gold Mining Industry* (1999) ISBN 1-874864-91-8

16. *Borderline Farming: Foreign Migrants in South African Commercial Agriculture* (2000) ISBN 1-874864-97-7

17. *Writing Xenophobia: Immigration and the Press in Post-Apartheid South Africa* (2000) ISBN 1-919798-01-3

18. *Losing Our Minds: Skills Migration and the South African Brain Drain* (2000) ISBN 1-919798-03-x

19. *Botswana: Migration Perspectives and Prospects* (2000) ISBN 1-919798-04-8

20. *The Brain Gain: Skilled Migrants and Immigration Policy in Post-Apartheid South Africa* (2000) ISBN 1-919798-14-5

21. *Cross-Border Raiding and Community Conflict in the Lesotho-South African Border Zone* (2001) ISBN 1-919798-16-1

22. *Immigration, Xenophobia and Human Rights in South Africa* (2001) ISBN 1-919798-30-7

23. *Gender and the Brain Drain from South Africa* (2001) ISBN 1-919798-35-8

24. *Spaces of Vulnerability: Migration and HIV/AIDS in South Africa* (2002) ISBN 1-919798-38-2

25. *Zimbabweans Who Move: Perspectives on International Migration in Zimbabwe* (2002) ISBN 1-919798-40-4

26. *The Border Within: The Future of the Lesotho-South African International Boundary* (2002) ISBN 1-919798-41-2

27. *Mobile Namibia: Migration Trends and Attitudes* (2002) ISBN 1-919798-44-7

28. *Changing Attitudes to Immigration and Refugee Policy in Botswana* (2003) ISBN 1-919798-47-1

29. *The New Brain Drain from Zimbabwe* (2003) ISBN 1-919798-48-X

30. *Regionalizing Xenophobia? Citizen Attitudes to Immigration and Refugee Policy in Southern Africa* (2004) ISBN 1-919798-53-6

31. *Migration, Sexuality and HIV/AIDS in Rural South Africa* (2004) ISBN 1-919798-63-3

32. *Swaziland Moves: Perceptions and Patterns of Modern Migration* (2004) ISBN 1-919798-67-6

33. *HIV/AIDS and Children's Migration in Southern Africa* (2004) ISBN 1-919798-70-6

34. *Medical Leave: The Exodus of Health Professionals from Zimbabwe* (2005) ISBN 1-919798-74-9

35. *Degrees of Uncertainty: Students and the Brain Drain in Southern Africa* (2005) ISBN 1-919798-84-6

36. *Restless Minds: South African Students and the Brain Drain* (2005) ISBN 1-919798-82-X

37. *Understanding Press Coverage of Cross-Border Migration in Southern Africa since 2000* (2005) ISBN 1-919798-91-9

38. *Northern Gateway: Cross-Border Migration Between Namibia and Angola* (2005) ISBN 1-919798-92-7

39. *Early Departures: The Emigration Potential of Zimbabwean Students* (2005) ISBN 1-919798-99-4

40. *Migration and Domestic Workers: Worlds of Work, Health and Mobility in Johannesburg* (2005) ISBN 1-920118-02-0

41. *The Quality of Migration Services Delivery in South Africa* (2005) ISBN 1-920118-03-9

42. *States of Vulnerability: The Future Brain Drain of Talent to South Africa* (2006) ISBN 1-920118-07-1

43. *Migration and Development in Mozambique: Poverty, Inequality and Survival* (2006) ISBN 1-920118-10-1

44. *Migration, Remittances and Development in Southern Africa* (2006) ISBN 1-920118-15-2

45. *Medical Recruiting: The Case of South African Health Care Professionals* (2007) ISBN 1-920118-47-0

46. *Voices From the Margins: Migrant Women's Experiences in Southern Africa* (2007) ISBN 1-920118-50-0

47. *The Haemorrhage of Health Professionals From South Africa: Medical Opinions* (2007) ISBN 978-1-920118-63-1

48. *The Quality of Immigration and Citizenship Services in Namibia* (2008) ISBN 978-1-920118-67-9

49. *Gender, Migration and Remittances in Southern Africa* (2008) ISBN 978-1-920118-70-9

50. *The Perfect Storm: The Realities of Xenophobia in Contemporary South Africa* (2008) ISBN 978-1-920118-71-6

51. *Migrant Remittances and Household Survival in Zimbabwe* (2009) ISBN 978-1-920118-92-1

52. *Migration, Remittances and 'Development' in Lesotho* (2010) ISBN 978-1-920409-26-5

53. *Migration-Induced HIV and AIDS in Rural Mozambique and Swaziland* (2011) ISBN 978-1-920409-49-4

54. *Medical Xenophobia: Zimbabwean Access to Health Services in South Africa* (2011) ISBN 978-1-920409-63-0

55. *The Engagement of the Zimbabwean Medical Diaspora* (2011) ISBN 978-1-920409-64-7

56. *Right to the Classroom: Educational Barriers for Zimbabweans in South Africa* (2011) ISBN 978-1-920409-68-5

57. *Patients Without Borders: Medical Tourism and Medical Migration in Southern Africa* (2012) ISBN 978-1-920409-74-6

58. *The Disengagement of the South African Medical Diaspora* (2012) ISBN 978-1-920596-00-2

59. *The Third Wave: Mixed Migration from Zimbabwe to South Africa* (2012) ISBN 978-1-920596-01-9

60. *Linking Migration, Food Security and Development* (2012) ISBN 978-1-920596-02-6

61. *Unfriendly Neighbours: Contemporary Migration from Zimbabwe to Botswana* (2012) ISBN 978-1-920596-16-3

62. *Heading North: The Zimbabwean Diaspora in Canada* (2012) ISBN 978-1-920596-03-3

63. *Dystopia and Disengagement: Diaspora Attitudes Towards South Africa* (2012) ISBN 978-1-920596-04-0

64. *Soft Targets: Xenophobia, Public Violence and Changing Attitudes to Migrants in South Africa after May 2008* (2013) ISBN 978-1-920596-05-7

65. *Brain Drain and Regain: Migration Behaviour of South African Medical Professionals* (2014) ISBN 978-1-920596-07-1

66. *Xenophobic Violence in South Africa: Denialism, Minimalism, Realism* (2014) ISBN 978-1-920596-08-8

67. *Migrant Entrepreneurship Collective Violence and Xenophobia in South Africa* (2014) ISBN 978-1-920596-09-5

Printed in the United States
By Bookmasters